Listen First–Sell Later

A Sales and Marketing Guide for Everyone!

Bob Poole

Edited by Megan Elizabeth Morris
www.worldmegan.net

Cover design by Paul Durban
www.blazonfire.com

First published in 2009 by Liverpool Press
Robert W. Poole
First Edition

ISBN 978-0-9824208-0-5

Library of Congress Control Number: 2009902952

To

Mom and Dad,
who started me down the path.

Joann,
who will always be.

and

Mindy and Ryan,
who inspire me every day.

Listen First–Sell Later

Introduction

This is a book for people who sell (whether they know it or not).

It's for people who own their own business and people who are just starting out. It's a book about communication and relationships, which means that you can use it to connect with your customers, bosses, employees, children, and parents, too. If you volunteer for a cause you're passionate about, or if you've got a great idea but you don't know how to start marketing it, this book will help you.

This book is for entrepreneurs, politicians, venture capitalists, students, job-seekers, and retirees looking for a new beginning.

In short, it's a sales and marketing book for *everyone*–because every one of us is selling and marketing all the time. Any time you try to persuade someone else to your point of view, you are selling something. Any time you need to get your message across to others, you're a marketer.

Even if you aren't a professional salesperson, your livelihood, even your quality of life, may depend on how well you sell. And it will almost *certainly* depend on the substance and quality of your interactions and relationships with other people–your ability to listen.

That's why this book is for you.

Listen First–Sell Later

In 1971, after working as a photojournalist, I decided to open a studio based photography business. I was very young and was under the impression that if I built a really great studio along with creating and presenting great work, the public would be knocking down my door. It didn't work like that.

I quickly realized that people were not ready to listen to what I had to say about my photography. It was only after I realized I had to get their attention first that I began to experience success.

As I got more experience in marketing and sales, this is what I learned: In order to get people to listen to what I had to say and buy what I had to sell, **I had to listen to them first**. I learned the value of asking questions and listening before trying to sell or market. I realized that attempting to sell something without listening to my customers *first* would be the same thing as a physician prescribing a drug without ever talking to the patient. I would be guilty of malpractice.

Many people today are starting their own small businesses for a number of reasons. Some do so because they're tired of the corporate grind. Others want to be their own boss, either as a second career or a precaution against downsizing. But unless they have a good background in sales and marketing, many of them will fail because they don't know how to get people's attention. They don't know that they need to listen first and sell later.

This book contains over 35 years of sales and marketing experience for people just like them—especially those just starting out or struggling. That's another thing I learned the hard way over many years: It's far easier to learn from other people's mistakes than your own. This way, you can learn from mine.

Listen with Your Eyes and Heart

Let's say you're at a party and it's a good networking opportunity. How long do you think the average person takes to make a decision about someone they've just met? How long does it take for your gut to say, "I like this person?" or "Wow, get me out of here!" If you're like most people you'll have that gut feeling within the first few minutes–sometimes less.

How do you come to a decision about someone else? Is it their dress, the tone or volume of their voice, the words they use, mannerisms, their smile, eye contact (or lack thereof)? Do they look around the room as you're being introduced, or do they make you feel like they're truly interested in you?

All of these things are part of the way we make a first impression. There are several ways you can take advantage of this. For one thing, learn how to match someone's tone and pace of speech. If you are caffeine-fueled, bouncing on the balls of your feet and speaking at warp speed, you're not going to connect with a calm, contemplative person who really thinks about each sentence. (In fact, they may well hate you.) Learn to use positive psychological reciprocity: Respond to another's positive action with one of your own. If your new acquaintance smiles, smile back. Watch them to keep it going.

These are ways to engender good will and trust. People do business with others they like and trust. Nurture a relationship with a client or potential client just like you would with someone you want to date.

Listen to them with your eyes and with your heart.

You Don't Understand Me

It's a teenager's favorite accusation when talking to their parents: "You don't understand me." What happens when we "grow up" and become adults? Do we sometimes still feel like people don't understand us? And whose fault is it?

If you're the speaker in a conversation, it's your responsibility to make sure the listener understands. On the other hand, if you are the listener, the responsibility falls upon you. It's actually a fifty-fifty process but the irony is that *100% of the responsibility is on both people.*

Let's talk about listeners. Listening is an art. The first thing you need to do is to tune the world out. Don't let your mind wander. Don't start thinking about your response until you know that you fully understand what the speaker is saying.

Make eye contact. And remember—you can only really look into one eye at a time. (I know that everyone talks about looking into a person's eyes, but if you try to look into both eyes at once, you'll give them a cross-eyed stare and probably get dizzy. Focus on one eye.)

Be aware of your body language. Don't crowd someone or get too casual, but try not to be too stiff or formal. Relax and smile and let them talk.

Give positive feedback if you understand what they're saying. Nod your head. Respond verbally with phrases like, "I see," "I understand," "I understand how you must feel." Feedback goes a long way toward meeting your 100% responsibility. Stop and ask for clarification if you don't understand.

If you give these a try, you'll find that speakers will respond much better to you—especially when you change roles, and you are the speaker.

Understand?

We're Talking but Not Listening

The entire process of communicating—talking, listening, understanding—is the foundation for all marketing and sales.

Without successful two-way communication, your marketing and sales efforts will be totally ineffective.

My friend Dennis once told me he was having a problem with a long-time client. They'd had a difference of opinion, and had eventually stopped talking. The client was still doing business with the firm, but Dennis and he still weren't talking.

Then one day Dennis told me they had started talking again. "We had a meeting earlier this week," he said.

"So, you resolved your problem?" I asked.

"No," Dennis said. "We're just ignoring it. But we are talking."

I agree with Dennis, they are talking–but they aren't communicating. Communicating requires both parties to listen and understand what the other person is saying. In this instance, talking but not listening to how both people feel about the original problem is likely to lead to further dissonance.

If establishing a business relationship is like dating, then maintaining a positive relationship is similar to maintaining a healthy marriage. All relationships experience conflict. How we deal with that conflict will determine the viability of our relationships–business and personal.

Communication requires good transmission skills. Too often we believe that we're making our point, and all the while our listener is hearing something totally different. Frustration escalates on everyone's part when the listener responds to what they *thought* they heard (or interpreted).

As the listener, it's your job to be absolutely certain that you understand what the speaker is saying. You need to communicate that understanding back to the speaker. Then, change roles.

If you still feel like you're not being understood, or that you don't understand what you've heard, you may need a third party to help. Better to engage a coach or consultant to assist you than to allow a good relationship to deteriorate.

Better Than Being Scratched By a Cat

When it comes to house pets, it seems like most people claim either to be cat people or dog people. Some, like me, are both.

It wasn't always that way. Once, I would have said I was a dog person. But a few years ago I was adopted by an older male cat that someone had "dumped" in the woods near a walking path I follow. I named him Walker and he quickly decided that I was his best friend. When Walker unexpectedly died 2 years ago, my wife and I rescued three other cats to join our two dog family.

Even at that point, I still wouldn't have called myself a cat person. I liked them, but I was a little afraid of them. They had all those claws and sharp teeth, and they knew how to use them! I'd give them some pats on the head and a few rubs but I was very careful to stay out of reach of those claws.

I'm telling you this today because all that has changed. As I sat down to write just now, two of the cats climbed up on me and my keyboard. This happens all the time. I rub them all over and they in turn roll over on their backs to have their stomachs rubbed. Quite frankly, there's a mutual love-in every morning at my desk!

What's changed? The answer is a single word: TRUST.

I trust them and they trust me. I have earned their trust, and they have earned mine.

Trust isn't something you can buy. It's not easy to earn, and it is easy to lose. In a world where buyers have an abundance of companies, products, and services to choose from, trust is scarce and valuable. More than that, trust increases in value as you nurture it–and as others throw theirs away. (Think of Wall Street, George W. Bush, the U.S. Department of Treasury... You get the idea.)

One way you can build trust is by listening. You can't sell to some-one without listening first. People won't trust you if they feel like you don't listen to them. Your employees won't trust you if they see that you're more concerned with the bottom line than their trust in you. The level of trust a leader can expect to receive is directly related to the follower's perception of the leader's respect, empathy, integrity, generosity, listening and communication skills.

How important is trust? It's the difference between hearing the sound of contented purring and getting your hands scratched and bit.

Trust is what makes everyone feel more invested and committed to each other. It is the most important intangible asset you have with your customers and clients.

You might want to spend more time on earning and building trust these days... and less on the things that anyone can copy.

Stop Selling

Customers and prospects know their problems much better than you do. Don't make the mistake of thinking that you already have the solutions. To assume you know the solution before you really understand the problem, once again, is like a physician writing a prescription before making a diagnosis.

Likewise, remember that positive customer relationships are not just about getting paid. The prospect might not need what you're selling–this time. But if you *do* know how to solve their problem (even if it doesn't mean a sale for you) don't you owe it to them to provide that solution? Would you rather be thought of as the salesperson who sells (insert anything here) or as the person who solves problems, regardless of your reward? Helping people only when you are getting paid falls short of best sales practices–and best life practices.

One of my first jobs was selling copiers for 3M at a time when Xerox–their competitor–was at its height in popularity. 3M was still focused on selling coated paper machines when Xerox had plain paper. (Plain paper cost the customer less than a penny a copy, while coated paper copies could cost as much as ten cents.) I learned very quickly that if all I did was sell copiers I was going to lose almost every time.

Instead, I established relationships with prospects. I asked questions about their lives, hobbies, goals, you name it. I shared the same kind of information about myself. And then I went about becoming a solutions provider. Any one individual solution might not have a thing to do with copiers. It might have to do with providing an introduction to a business client. Sometimes it meant telling them I couldn't help them this time and I'd give them the name of a competitor.

Regardless, I would stay in touch. And when they needed another copier or knew someone who did, I most often got the call. I broke every sales record for the company my first year. What's more, I did it in a territory that was considered to be economically depressed–a territory nobody else wanted.

Stop being a salesperson. Become a solutions provider. You'll be much more productive.

It's more fun.

And, it's the right thing to do.

Change Happens

People buy for their own reasons–not for yours.

(That includes voters.)

It's not enough that you know all the reasons why someone should want to buy what you're selling. It's not enough to throw advertisement after advertisement at them without knowing their reasons for buying. And, quite often, the reasons why they bought what you (or your political party) were selling the last time they bought–changes.

Things happen to alter their view and their viewpoints. One day Walker came into my life by accident, and all my thinking about cats changed. Everyone is affected by events like this (even when it's not about a cat!), and everyone changes. When your long-time customers experience change in their lives, you'd better be on top of what they're experiencing. The same old story isn't likely to get their attention.

You have to learn their reasons for buying–ask them. You don't need to persuade them or "sell them." They'll sell themselves if they see you as the person who best understands their needs and can do something about it.

They buy because of what they believe you will do for them.

Our Customers Want Belly Rubs

The dogs and cats I live with bring me so much joy–watching them live in the moment has, frankly, taught me more about life than I ever learned in school.

Today my youngest dog, Bucca, taught me another lesson. He loves to have his belly rubbed. Three or four times a day I'll hear the jingling of his collar tags as he makes his way up several flights of stairs to my third floor office. His sole purpose for these visits, as far as I can tell, is to have me rub his belly.

Recently, I was reading a blog entry by Seth Godin about "Customers That Care"[1] when Bucca made the trip to my office. Bucca whined, barked and pawed at my legs until I gave in and proceeded to rub his belly. Seth's article, coincidentally, was about the importance of getting customers to care about our business–and then actually listening to them.

Think about it. Our customers also want us to give them belly rubs! I'm not suggesting you actually rub their bellies, although such a movement might make for a kinder, more civilized society. But think of belly rubs as paying attention to and communicating with your customers, and letting them know you appreciate them.

You know yourself how good it feels to get a massage, especially when you've had a tough day. You could make someone feel wonderful by showing that you appreciate them. You could change their entire outlook for that moment–or more–just by giving them that attention.

Business is about relationships.

Customers want belly rubs!

We're All Connected In Some Way

As I began writing this book, an image of how I learned the value of relationships in business came flooding into my mind. I couldn't help but smile at the memory.

I was a brand new Major Account Sales Executive for 3M Company. I had just been promoted after several years in their employ, and I was expected to call on major accounts–but primarily ones where we'd never had any business. This essentially meant that I had to go out and find new customers in larger companies with more gatekeepers and bureaucracy!

One of the accounts I was expected to "open" was a steel company headquartered near my home town. It turned out there was one man whose

---

[1]http://sethgodin.typepad.com/seths_blog/2008/01/customers-that.html

primary job was to manage the copier equipment and supply program for the entire company. His name was Frank.

Did you ever meet someone and instantly know there was going to be mutual loathing between the two of you? That was Frank and I. It took us both about 10 seconds to make our determination.

As far as I could see, Frank was the kind of person who plodded though life all wrapped up in habit, routine and insignificant details. Since I was very driven (probably called Type A at the time), I found *everything Frank did* to be frustrating. I would ask him a question, and I'd wait for the answer. Then I'd wait some more.

Frank would pull a pipe out of a holster he carried on his belt and begin the process of filling and lighting it. Since that took at least five minutes, I was on to the next question since I assumed he'd forgotten the first one. Just about the time I was on my fourth or fifth question without an answer, Frank would respond to the first question–which led to more frustration and loathing on my part. And so it went every single time I paid a call on Frank. I was getting nowhere and I dreaded having to go see him.

Then one day, I stopped at a drug store near his office. While at the cash register, I saw a display of corn cob pipes. They were inexpensive, so I picked one out and then picked out a bag of pipe tobacco that looked familiar to me. I stuck them in my suit pockets and made a resolution: When Frank went to light up, I'd do the same. Maybe if we had pipe smoking in common he'd find me more acceptable.

The meeting began as before, only *this* time I pulled out my pipe and tobacco when Frank went for his. It was the most animation I had seen from the man in months. He said, "I didn't know you smoked a pipe."

"I haven't for long," I told him. I asked him about the tobacco I had picked out, and whether he liked it. He went on to tell me more about tobacco and pipes than anyone, in my mind, would want to ever know– over the next two hours! It turned out he blended his own tobacco and he told me mine was junk with perfume added to make it smell good. He had me dump it and gave me some of his private blend. We smoked pipes and got to know one another.

Over the next few months we found out we had a lot more in common than we did in differences. It turned out we had both grown up in the same little Ohio town that I had left years before; he had lived there his whole life. When we started comparing notes we found out we knew a lot of the same people. Apparently my younger brother had dated his daughter for a while! (I was worried when I heard that, but it turned out fine.) We started meeting for lunch. He always had lunch at his desk so on the days we had a meeting scheduled, he packed a sandwich for me. One day down the road, after a few pipes, sandwiches and meetings, Frank said: "I guess we ought to talk about copiers."

We talked, and he bought. I finished the year as one of the Top Ten Sales Executives in the United States for 3M. Frank's company's business was one of the major contributing factors to my success.

It's all about the relationship–the connection we have as human beings. I had figured out that if I wanted to communicate with Frank and have any kind of business relationship (which was the whole idea); I was going to have to learn how to communicate with him in a way that made him comfortable. Talking at 500 words a minute and *interrogating* him before he liked and trusted me was never going to work with Frank. It isn't going to work very often with any of your clients either.

The next time you're having a problem establishing a relationship with someone, think about Frank and our pipe smoking. Find some common ground. Focus on your relationship with that person–not your services or products. Don't interrogate people. Learn to match the pace and tone of their speech. If they speak slowly and softly and you speak quickly and loudly, slow down and lower the volume. Put them at ease and get them talking about themselves, the things you have in common. Most people like to talk about their families and what they do in their spare time. People have to "buy you" before they buy anything *from* you.

The Greatest Life Insurance Salesman in the World

I grew up in a small town on the Ohio River called East Liverpool. It's located in Ohio, at the junction of Ohio, Pennsylvania and West Virginia.

When I was growing up it had a population of about 22,000. Today the population has dropped to just over 13,000. Don't let that fool you–some very unique and notable people have come from my town. This is a story about one who learned the meaning of providing value for his clients so well that he went on to become the greatest life insurance salesman in the world.

His name was Ben Feldman (1912–1993). In his fifty years of selling insurance for one company, his sales volume exceeded $1.8 billion. Over a third of that volume came after he turned 65. He did it by selling out of his office in East Liverpool (certainly not a major financial center like New York).

Now you might be thinking to yourself that Ben must have been some kind of superstar: A good looking, fast talking kind of man (but you'd be wrong). Ben was short, stout, and balding. He spoke slowly, with a distinct lisp. He never finished high school. He was so shy that years later when he was asked to speak at insurance industry meetings, he would only agree if a screen was erected between him and the audience.

But Ben was a *legend* when it came to one thing. He made a point to know every business owner in his region. He did his homework first and learned all he could about his potential customers. By the time he met with them (often on a cold call) he was ready with just the right value development questions. He didn't always sell right away, but he never gave up. I once heard him say that for years, he wouldn't stop working for that day until he'd made at least one sale–no matter how late it got.

One of my favorite stories is about Ben's relationship with a prominent real estate developer. Ben tried for weeks to get in to see him but was always unsuccessful; the man was just too busy! One day, Ben stopped in cold and handed the developer's assistant an envelope with five $100 bills and asked her to give it to her boss. He told her "If I don't have a good idea for him, he can keep the money." He got in and sold a $14 million policy. Years later when Ben realized the developer needed additional insurance due to the unprecedented growth of his company; he was once again stymied by the man's insistence that he was too busy to take a physical. Undaunted, Ben rented a fully equipped mobile hospital van, hired a doctor and sent them along. Rumor is that the man ended up with over $50 million in coverage.

In 1992, New York Life marked Ben's 50th year with the company by proclaiming "Feldman's February," a national sales competition. Ben took this as a personal challenge. The winner of the contest (at 80 years old) was Ben Feldman.

Ben was famous for his sayings that he used to inspire both clients and himself. My favorite is:

> "Doing something costs something.
> Doing nothing costs something.
> And quite often, doing nothing costs a lot more."

Ben Feldman died in 1993 at 81. A few years before his death he was asked about the largest policy that he had ever written. "I can't say. I haven't written it yet."

Charisma Is Overrated; Integrity Is Better

When I first started hiring salespeople, I was often swayed by those who possessed a lot of charisma. I assumed if you were charismatic you had a better chance of opening doors and attracting attention.

I was correct. Charisma can open doors for you.

But, alas—you need more than charisma to be a successful salesperson. You need a strong sense of responsibility for your own success. That means you have to work hard with high personal integrity.

There are a number of other qualities the best salespeople enjoy and we could argue about which is the most important. But charisma isn't it.

The qualities you're looking for aren't on the outside. The most important qualities in sales are the ones *inside the person*.

I'll take integrity over charisma, every time.

How to Change Your Life

Don't read this if you're completely satisfied with your life. I'm addressing only those people who still have dreams—and want to make their dreams come true. If you're satisfied with your life and you're living your dreams and have met all your goals, you might want to go to the next story. But I'm guessing if you're like most people, you still have some dreams left to be fulfilled.

So how do we turn dreams into reality?

First, what you *don't* do: You *don't* sit around visualizing. "Sit" is the key word. Don't sit! Making your dreams come true takes *action*. There's nothing wrong with visualizing what you want—professional athletes, artists, and performers do it all the time. But, they also **practice, practice, and practice some more** so they can turn the visualized dream into a dream come true.

Here's the short list on how to make your dreams come true:

1. Goals—yep, you've heard it all before. Do you set goals? Do you write them down and carry them with you all the time? Ask the top achievers in any field, and I bet you'll find out that's exactly what they do. Set goals. Write them down.

2. Review your goals all the time and keep them updated. Life changes. You'll change, and so will your goals.

3. Make some big, lifetime goals. I have my list—it's amazing what happens when you write them down. Things you thought were far-off dreams just a few years ago come true more quickly than you might realize.

4. Now that you have your goals, you need to break each one down into the things you need to accomplish to meet the goal. Let's say you want to lose 25 pounds. You'll have to make a plan for your diet and exercise. You'll need to track what you eat and how much you work out. Want to learn how to speak Italian? The plan is easy; you'll need lessons. But how will you learn? Will you hire a tutor,

take classes, or learn by self-study? Or maybe you'll live in Italy for a year!

5. You have the goals and the plan—**now just go do it.** It's that simple. Well, not that simple—it requires sacrifice and persistence. If your dreams are really big, you'll find all kinds of reasons to quit. Plenty of people who have given up on their dreams will try and tell you why you should, too. But action is the key. **You have to do the work.**

It's your life to make into what you wish. Time isn't an issue. You have all there is to have. Only two things can hold you back:

1. Lack of belief in yourself.

2. Lack of action.

Come on—what do you really want? What do you really want to do in your lifetime? Write it down. Share it with your best friend.

I promise you it will be life changing.

One Person Can Make the Difference

I recently spent time with a group of wonderful volunteers at a private school[2] where I am a trustee. These people all have children who attend that same school and they're passionate about letting other people know about it.

I don't have any children in the school, or any affiliation with them. Last year a good friend's son asked me to come to Grandparents Day to stand in for his grandparents. I spent half a day with them, and I was blown away! This school truly understands education as it was intended to be. The kids are engaged, passionate and love learning there, and I heard this from the kids themselves. The teachers and administrators are true leaders, and they love showing their students how to break the status quo. I had to be a part of it—so I asked them how I could help. I'm having a ball!

A couple of months ago I created a Ning[3] social network for the school in a matter of hours. A project like this would have taken weeks of coding

[2]United Friends School: http://www.unitedfriendsschool.org/
[3]Ning, create your own social network: http://www.ning.com/

and lots of dollars to produce from scratch, and that would have been my only option not too long ago. The cost was zero.

We are living in a time when one person can make a big impact on the lives of others clearly, quickly and easily. The tools we have available are unlike those of any other time in history. With these technologies, there are only two requirements left: It still takes the desire to make a difference and faith that you can.

Seth Godin coined the term "sheepwalking" to describe people who are complacent, stuck in the status quo.[4] If you're reading this book, you're not likely to be a sheepwalker. You might have the desire you need, or you might be on hold, wondering if you can be a successful business owner or entrepreneur.

Have faith–you can do it. Faith is where it all starts.

Jump Start

Here's an idea that should give you a jump start going forward: For the next three months spend as much time as possible learning about one industry or type of business you'd like to focus your sales and marketing efforts upon.

Set two goals:

1. Learn as much about that particular type of business or industry as any "insider."

2. Develop a product, tool, system, or service that will address the greatest business challenge that chosen business or industry faces.

You might have to spend some nights or weekends doing this. But, if you do, two things will happen:

1. You will be perceived as an expert in the industry and you'll know more than the competition.

2. You will have something new and exciting to market and sell that nobody else has.

---

[4]Seth Godin used the term "sheepwalking" in his book *Tribes: We Need You to Lead Us.*

Oh and there is a third thing—the next month, quarter, or year will be more exciting, productive, and profitable for you.

If You Had a Crystal Ball

The current economic craziness is going to be a catalyst for many people to make the jump from working for someone else to working for themselves. Some will not have many other choices and others will do it because they have decided not to let their futures be determined by factors other than their own initiative and hard work.

What if you had a crystal ball that could tell you what kind of business-es would be best to consider? The slate is clean and you can pick anything. What type of businesses would be best to consider in a down economy?

Here are some ideas:

- Pampering personal services like massage and spas. (Don't forget services like these for men.)

- Coaching, mentoring, consulting and job retraining.

- Internet businesses.

- Counseling or self-help services on how to make and save money.

- Home repair and home landscaping including hard-scape, lighting, and comfort and aesthetics.

- Security—especially home security.

- Alcohol, wine, gambling and other "vices"—you can imagine!

- Luxury goods at all levels. People want to feel comforted.

- Pain Management.

- Health care.

- Pet care and anything to do with pets.

- Elderly care, and anything that the boomers will need over the next twenty years.

Remember that you can make more money–but you can't buy more time. Think about other types of businesses that allow people to enjoy their time more, especially the time spent with family and friends.

Ready, Set, Whoa!

You're ready to make the move to your own business. You know what you want to do, you're passionate about it, and you're ready to make the time commitment.

Stop! If this is your first time, you need to ask yourself some questions:

1. Do I have enough money? What if I'm wrong and I need more? Where will I get it?

2. Should I bootstrap a little bit at a time and keep working my other job, or jump in with both feet?

3. If I don't have another job, should I consider getting one before taking this step?

4. Who else is hurt if I fail? Do I have enough money for living expenses for the next six months? The next year?

5. Who should I trust for advice? (My experience is that accountants and attorneys make good accountants and attorneys. Don't expect them to advise you in business strategies, tactics, sales, marketing, etc. Find successful business people and ask them if you can interview them. Tell them why and what you're planning. Most will be very willing to talk with you. Trust but verify.)

6. Where do I go for marketing advice? (The answer: Not the local newspaper, radio, TV or Yellow Book account person. Buy books on marketing and sales. Take a sales training course. Find a consultant who has a successful track record. Run from anyone who tells you advertising is the solution!)

7. Where do I go to learn how to write a business plan? (That's easy you don't need a formal business plan. They're useless by the time you execute, if not before. You need a marketing plan, and you need to know when to abandon the plan... or change direction.)

8. What else do I need to consider?

There are probably at least 100 other things. But, these are the questions that I'd want my best friend to think about first!

Lastly, realize that you don't have all the answers. None of us do. Ask for help–especially when you think you don't need it.

25 (More) Questions to Consider

1. What is the purpose of your company? (Just one sentence.)

2. What are three words that describe your company?

3. What companies would you like to emulate?

4. What are the most compelling aspects of the product or service your company offers?

5. What business and consumer trends will affect your business going forward?

6. What are the advantages to your customers if they buy from you instead of the competition?

7. Describe what your company will look like five years from now.

8. What is important about the history and background of your company's owners?

9. Describe the perfect prospect for your products and services. Tell me their average age, what kinds of restaurants they visit, and vacation spots. What do we need to know about them as people that you think might be important?

10. How would you finish this statement? "I'd like my company to be more..."

11. How would you finish this statement? "I'd like my company to be less..."

12. What is your company's number one goal for the coming year?

13. What do you believe will be the greatest obstacle to your future success?

14. What do you believe is the greatest immediate opportunity for your company?

15. What do you think is your company's greatest long-term opportunity?

16. What do you personally have to do, change, or commit to in order to meet your goals and take advantage of those opportunities?

17. Have you made a commitment, or are you still analyzing?

18. What are the customer's key criteria in choosing (whatever it is you're selling)?

19. How will you know when your company's results have met your expectations? How will you measure it?

20. What if this fails?

21. What will you do to you keep it from failing?

22. Have you considered what you're willing to spend to meet your goals?

23. Have any resources already been allocated?

24. Who else could benefit from considering these questions?

25. What are you going to do with your answers?

You Made a What?

Did you ever meet someone who says they wouldn't change anything in their career?

Anyone who says they haven't made mistakes or hasn't failed is a person not to be trusted.

Any boss who won't let their employees fail is a boss who will have employees who don't try to do the right things–or, new things.

They are frauds or incompetent or both.

Life is too enjoyable to deal with either one.

Small Business Land Mines

I've been working with small businesses and entrepreneurial start-ups for much of my life. There are some wonderful rewards and benefits in seeing something grow. There are also some potential land mines that too many small, family owned businesses run into that lead to problems, lost revenues and, sometimes, lost companies.

One of the land mines that I see 80% of the time is that small business owners often equate prior success in another business, sports, etc., to believing that he or she is accomplished in regards to running the current business. This keeps many a person from hiring experts outside their own field. I can't tell you how many times I've been contacted after companies have tried to run their own sales and marketing programs, only to have failed. They never have a marketing plan, which should have come first. They don't know how to create one and they don't understand the value and necessity of having one. If they do have a marketing plan, it's sitting in a three-ring binder in a desk drawer that never gets opened.

Decisions tend to be emotional and not based on reason in small businesses. If you were running a "big business" you would be thinking big and have a different mindset. It's hard for small business people to think this way because their decisions are often compared against personal or family needs. There's often a spouse or other relative that influences decision making, yet knows almost nothing about the things one would need to know to make a rational business decision.

In fact, I've often experienced situations where one member of the family is purposefully sabotaging the business. You think that sounds unlikely–not in the least bit. I've seen a spouse create turmoil and drive employees and customers away because they wanted the attention their spouse was giving the company. I've seen one son engage in lying, cheating and stealing because he was jealous of his siblings. I could go on but please know it could be happening in your small business and you won't know it until it's too late.

Because there's often a distrust of outsiders; advice from consultants, accountants and attorneys is often ignored or only partially implemented. Sometimes I feel like a physician whose patient tells him, "I decided to only take half of the prescription because I was feeling better," only to have the patient get worse and need more drastic intervention. Again, recognize you can't have all the answers and you must trust and rely upon others who are more qualified in their particular area of business.

So what can you as a small business owner do to avoid some of these land mines?

1. First, focus on making decisions rationally. Assume you are a CEO of a large company and **do the right thing**. Don't get caught up in "doing things right"–which often means "the way we've always done them."

2. Hire good advisers. Nobody has all the answers in a small company. Make sure your advisers have the skills and experience to really help you. My experience is that too many small business owners ask their accountants or attorneys for business advice. Accountants and attorneys are usually good accountants and attorneys, but are rarely good business advisors.

3. If other family members are actively involved in the company make sure they have the same accountability an outside employee would have in the position. Treat them honestly and fairly as you should any employee, and not like "one of the family."

4. Make sure your spouse and other family members are "on the same page" in regards to everyone's role in regards to the company. Even

if they're not active in the company they can be passively affecting it in a negative or positive way. Make sure it is the latter!

5. Start each day by asking yourself, "How can I provide value today for my clients and customers?" Focus on doing that, and many of the potential land mines will never enter your business life.

Believe me, it's more difficult to pick up the pieces and have to unwind and re-start–and always more expensive than getting good advice on how to avoid the land mines in the first place.

Everything Becomes Magnified

Everything becomes magnified when you're the business owner. Now you're the one who has to meet the payroll, make sure the clients are happy, maintain good relationships with your suppliers and distributors and be the Chief Marketing Officer. All these things get "bigger" when it's your company.

How do you handle them without working 70 hours or more every week? How do you maintain the kind of relationships you want and need with your spouse, family, and friends? How do you keep from dropping over at an early age because of stress?

My suggestion: Ignore people who tell you to compartmentalize your life. You know–that old saw about keeping your work separate from your home life. You won't be able to pull it off! In the end, your life outside of work will suffer. You don't have different lives. You have one life. Allow yourself, your family and friends to be part of it (all of it).

It's important to know how to deal with the emotional ups and downs of running a small business. We all know the usual tips about eating right and exercising. Here are a few more that might come in handy.

Don't allow yourself to become isolated from old friends. It's really easy to let this happen. I found myself seeing good friends less and less as I was building my first business. I didn't feel like we had as much in common as we once did. Allowing our connection to fade was a mistake.

Take the time to nurture those relationships for your emotional and mental well being.

Don't let minor problems and frustrations escalate into "big deals" that sap your energy. Breathe and let them go. Work at maintaining your perspective. This applies to people, too–I personally will not work with obsessively negative or passive aggressive people. I find them to be sucking black holes of energy and I stay as far away from them as possible!

Take time for yourself every day. Get away from your desk to think. Keep something with you to take notes with when you're hit with an inspiration.

Know when to ask for help. You don't always have to be right. You'll make mistakes. You need to concentrate on being right as much as possible about the things that really are a "big deal."

At Last, He Gets the Picture

I got a note yesterday from an acquaintance who's trying to break into the field of professional photography. He's young and has experience in photography, but he admits he's not a good "self marketer" and says he's suffering because of it.

His note got me to thinking about my own experience–under the same circumstances and almost forty years ago. That experience was life changing for me. Before I moved out of photojournalism, I was fed assignments by magazines, newspapers, and bureaus. As a studio owner, I had to manage the overhead of my own studio. I was a kid by today's standards and really had very little understanding of marketing. But *who cared*, I thought then. I was a very good photographer, and once people saw my work I was bound to be a success.

A little over a year later I had exhausted all my funds. While the business was growing every quarter, it wasn't growing fast enough for me to make a living right at that moment. With no access to money I might invest in the business, I quickly determined that I needed to learn how to be a marketer–and *fast!*

I had tried advertising before, and while it got me some name recognition and the occasional new customer, I knew that it took too long to produce results. In addition to that, the value of advertising was far less than the investment. I needed to find something that would get people talking and at the same time wouldn't cost much. Even better, I decided I needed to stir up word of mouth for my business... *and get paid to do it.*

When asked why he robbed banks, Willie Sutton said: "Because that's where the money is!"[5] I took a look at the newspaper and billboard advertisements of the largest local bank (the same one that handled my exhausted business loan), and paid attention to their radio spots. I decided that I could create a promotion for them that would be *better* than their advertising.

The next week, I made an appointment with the president and outlined a promotion that I called "Faces of the Tri-State Area." (This bank was in Ohio, on the border of Pennsylvania and West Virginia–hence the tri-state area.) I told him how I would go into local businesses, steel mills, potteries, schools, and churches–everywhere the bank's customers lived, worked and played–and that I would create vivid black & white portraits of the people I found there. I'd then enlarge, mat and frame them, and we'd hang the whole display in the bank's main lobby. At the same time, the bank would change their print and radio advertising to bring people in to see the gallery, all the while stressing that *their customers* are their most important asset–part of the theme.

He loved the idea and asked how much. I named a figure that, besides the photography, included building the gallery display and writing the advertising copy. It was a large number for me at the time, but they went with it and the show was a hit! Of course, my name was credited for the photography and the show, which brought in many new customers. I also got to make fantastic contacts at the local businesses where I did the photography, which led to more commercial business. Last but not least, I was stopped on the street about a month into the show by the chairman of the board of the local competing bank. He complimented me on the promotion and asked how it came to be. I told him the story, including my realization that I had to learn to market or starve. Later on he and his son

---

[5]Willie Sutton: http://en.wikipedia.org/wiki/Sutton%27s_law

became very influential in guiding more business my way–including that of his own bank.

This experience was the genesis for my transition into full-time marketing and sales consulting, as I gradually moved away from photography. I found I enjoyed the creativity of marketing; I was able to help more people be successful and I got to work "normal hours."

If you are starting a new business or one that's struggling to get to the next level, think about my story and ask yourself what you personally are doing to create marketing for your company. Don't rely on print media advertising. I know it's easy to have someone create an ad–all you have to do is write the check–but these days, it's almost always a waste of time. Remember: No matter what business you're in, you are *first and foremost* a marketer.

By the way... In 1970, Willie Sutton (the bank robber) did a television commercial to promote the New Britain, Connecticut Bank and Trust Company's new photo credit card program.

He had finally learned that it's *marketing* that pays–not crime.

Listen to the Experts

For some time now, I have been preaching that if you are a small business owner or a sales professional, you also need to be the Chief Marketing Officer. That hasn't changed in light of the current economy. It's even more important.

However, you need to realize that unless you have been trained and spent a bunch of years as a professional marketer, you probably don't know what to do. You might not have a strategy, or the one you have could be wrong. You might not understand what tactics to use. What's even worse– you might think because you're a smart person and understand (insert your profession, experience, past success here) that you can also "figure out" marketing for your own company. That's not likely unless you're a very rare person who has a natural affinity and talent for marketing. The emphasis is on rare!

Marketing tactics and mechanics can be learned from books, class-room, or even on-the-job training. But that just makes you a mechanic. **True marketing is also an art.**

You have a couple of choices. You can hire a professional marketer for your company. (Please don't hire anyone from an advertising agency without first knowing if they understand more than media placement and using advertising to drive business. There are plenty of agencies who do. There are more that don't.) Hiring someone in-house works only if you partner with them. You can't say to yourself, "I've got myself a marketing person" and then step back and wait for results. You are still the Chief Marketing Officer.

You can also get help from someone who consults in marketing. They can help you with strategy and process. You'll still need to execute but you'll have someone professional you can talk with and help keep you on the right track.

If you go that route, please listen to the person you hire and don't second guess everything. You're wasting time and money if you do. Business managers too often look for a "cure" and a quick one at that. Consultants don't offer cures. The good ones offer creative ideas based on knowledge, education and lots of experience. They offer a process that if followed, is likely to move you closer towards your business and personal goals.

Think about your situation. What are you doing that is remarkably different this year? How are you innovating? What are you doing to spread your story like a virus that is passed from person to person?

There is no safe haven. You can't hide, build a moat, or erect walls to keep out the competition. You can't halt the changes affecting today's marketing. Set the goals, get some help and get moving.

"I'm Not That Kind of Girl"

I got a referral call from Denise yesterday. She's a friend of one of my clients. Denise has been in a gift basket service business for almost two years, and she's thinking of giving up. Her business has been continually bleeding red ink, so she came to me looking for marketing help.

I asked what she personally has done so far to market her business. Her answer: It was the usual Yellow Page ad, business cards, brochure and some fliers passed out to offices in her area. She had also attended some women's networking events. She thought maybe she needed a website update.

"I'm really not the marketing type," she told me.

"If you really believe that," I said, "You aren't going to like what I have to say next!"

I told her that the *most important* job of a business owner is marketing. You can be the best in the world at what you do (in fact, that should be your goal), but if you aren't "that type" you just aren't going to make it in your own business.

There were a few seconds of silence on the phone.

"We need to talk then," she said finally, "because I think I *am* the best at what I do. I just need to figure out how to let others know that, too."

I asked her the following question: When considering all my other options (and her competitors' services), why should I buy from her?

Her response was a lot of "me too" answers—ones that apply to pretty much everyone in her field. So I asked her to tell me a story about the reason she got into her business in the first place. "You obviously feel passionate about what you do and what your customers say about why they come to you. Why?" I asked.

Now *that* was a start. She got the idea immediately, and we started talking about her unique story. **You need to have a story, too.** It has to answer the same question. Why should I buy from you when I have all the other choices in the world?

Oh yeah—and first you need to believe you *are* "that type." The marketing type!

Marketing, Not Prospecting

If you are in sales or own your own business, you must constantly be marketing. I'm not talking about prospecting; I gave that up about 25 years ago (I hated it). I gave it up because I'd determined that if I had a consistent marketing program, I would never have to prospect again! You want people to come to you because of referrals–and because you've created something remarkable, whether it's your product, service, or your entire company. That's what good marketing does.

Consistency is the key; even when you're busy doing everything else your job requires, you still have to be marketing. Take advantage of technology. Use e-newsletters, email, social networking tools, and public relations. Use some limited networking (but not so much that you neglect your business). Write thank you notes! Even with my terrible handwriting, I still send out notes on a regular basis. (In fact, I had my very best handwriting turned into a font that I can use on my computer to "handwrite" letters. Use the right printer and ink color and you'll come very close to handwritten–which is a blessing if your handwriting is as bad as mine! I used a company called FontGod[6] and they were fantastic with their service.)

Not all these things will be your cup of tea. For example, I hate formal networking events, though I have found some of them to be worthwhile. (With networking you need to do your homework ahead of time to find out who you want to meet. Meeting this person and beginning a relationship becomes your goal!) Your preferences will be different. In order to really be good at marketing, you can't stop learning. I notice that people who tell me they've never read a book or don't have time to learn about new technology tend to be out of touch with today's business reality. They're being left behind.

Get out of your own world. Start learning about social networking and how you can use it. Team up with someone else in business or sales, and brainstorm. Pick up a new magazine article or add a fresh technology to your arsenal.

[6]FontGod, make a font out of your handwriting: http://www.fontgod.com/

Too Many Hats?

If you're like most small business owners, you find that you wear a lot of different hats. One minute you're the CEO, then the head of sales, and often the person who cleans up at the end of the day.

Give serious thought to outsourcing those tasks.

I know it can be difficult to free up money to pay someone to do work that you can do just as well (or even better)—but there's a trap here you need to avoid. Too often, it's easier to stuff envelopes, do the accounting, run the errands and a dozen other things... and you forget to be the Chief Marketing Officer. Remember, your primary job as business owner is as head of marketing—when business is really good, when business is really bad, and *especially* when business is somewhere in-between.

With the time you free up from having someone else do those jobs, you can create a marketing system for a niche group you've wanted to approach. You can host a breakfast networking event, and invite a select group of decision makers. You can start writing that blog you *know* you need. You can learn how to *stop* trading hours for time, and start leveraging your business to increase revenues.

Instead of saving a few bucks by doing jobs you shouldn't be doing, you can focus on increasing business, which will pay for those services many times over. And you'll be building assets at the same time.

Every day you hesitate to let someone else do these tasks is a day you lose money and opportunities.

Personally, I hate losing. I bet you do, too.

Chicken or the Egg

I've heard many times over the years that the number one reason for a new company's failure is lack of capital. I'm not sure I agree based on my experience. Being well-capitalized is wonderful—if you can afford it. Many small companies, however, have been started with a great idea, a lot of passion and *zero* money. The one commonality? They almost *always* have great marketing.

Too many people have an idea and a passion (and even plenty of money), but *no clue* how to actually market and sell. They believe so much in what they're doing they feel like they can "will" their way to success. And don't get me wrong–sometimes if you have enough money and are willing to lose some while learning, you can do that.

I suggest you do things a little differently. If you've never actually sold anything or implemented successful marketing, study and get some help. Spend some time and money *before* you pull the trigger and open your business. Visit successful business owners and interview them. Ask them how they got to where they are today. Ask them how they learned about sales and marketing, and what they would have done differently. Buy the best business, sales and marketing books available. (Take a look at the list in the back of this book for some suggestions.) Plus, you probably won't start your new company without some legal and financial advice–promise yourself you'll get some professional sales and marketing advice too. You'll grow more quickly (with fewer growing pains).

How to Compete with Unlimited Competition

Thirty years ago, customers' choices were still limited by geography and availability. That is not the case today! Today your customers really *do* have unlimited access to the same product or service you are selling. It's all just a few clicks away on the web.

So what are you doing to differentiate your company, its products, and yourself? How do you compete with unlimited competition?

Here are three simple (yet difficult) questions to ask yourself. The answers can lead you to developing your Unique Selling Proposition–your individual story that tells why customers come to you instead of someone else. The right answers can mean the difference between extraordinary success... and barely getting by!

- Why should I choose to do business with you, versus any and every other option available to me?
- What do you offer that no one else can (or will)?
- What is your reason for existence in your chosen market–besides the fact that it's where you want to be?

How to Out-Market the Competition

In my work, I'm always amazed (but not surprised) at how many companies don't yet have a Unique Selling Proposition. Without having one (or without knowing you have one) you become just another commodity company–and you might as well make plans to sell out or close up. That's how important your USP is.

This applies to all businesses; it doesn't matter if you're a Fortune 100, professional practice, or a mom and pop retail store. You must have a USP! If you don't have one now, you can start by answering the three questions I asked a minute ago.

Your USP must always be stated as a **benefit** that your clients and customers can clearly identify with and agree upon in terms of its uniqueness and value to them. The long-term marketing and operational successes you achieve will ultimately be helped or hurt by the USP you decide upon.

Here's an example: "We will deliver any computer part in our catalog to you within 24 hours or you don't pay!"

This would be a powerful Unique Selling Proposition–and it would definitely set the company apart. The competition would have to scramble to keep up, and it would create the perception that this company is *the company* to do business with in that particular industry.

Instead of a great USP, most companies are saying "me too." These are commonplace, wishy-washy businesses feeding solely on the sheer momentum of the marketplace. When the momentum stops–so do they. There's nothing unique; there's nothing distinct. They promise no great value, benefit, or service–just "buy from us" for no justifiable, rational reason.

Do you like spending money with a firm that has no unique benefit, service, selection, guarantee–or anything else that sets it apart? I doubt it, which is why most people are more than willing to switch companies for little or no reason!

More than that, it's impossible to compete merely on price or service anymore. Customers have the internet on their side, and they can always get a better price (and better service) elsewhere. You must be unique and extraordinary, and you must be able to make that part of your overall company strategy.

On top of that, you must be able to *implement* that strategy. The *worst* thing you can do is fail to deliver on your finely-crafted USP. That's the kiss of death for many companies. It's just like having a beautiful strategy in a three ring binder in your desk drawer, but never putting it into action!

Take some time today and write down your Unique Selling Proposition. Then, without sharing what you wrote, ask your employees and co-workers what your company's USP is. I think you might be surprised at their answers. If you are, it's time to make sure every person in the company knows your USP and is focused on delivering it. I guarantee you will add considerable income to the company bottom line.

Whose Fault Is It?

If you keep saying the same things to the same people, sooner or later they'll tune you out. They'll go away.

Whose fault is it if they do?

Whose fault is it if they just don't understand your value proposition or why they should follow you? Whose fault is it if you keep telling them why they should do business with you–but they don't?

It's yours.

If you've failed to persuade them, it's your fault. Maybe it's you who needs to change. Maybe instead of trying to push and pull them into *your* world, you need to do a better job of listening and leading.

Maybe it's time to get really creative and do something that makes them *want* to follow you.

Blocking and Tackling

When you try to please everyone you're not going to be happy with the outcome. You can't do it. Likewise, when you try to market to everyone you're also setting yourself up for failure.

One of the more difficult challenges I face is convincing business owners to focus their sales and marketing efforts on people who actually want what it is they're selling. By doing this, they'd increase their odds of success, decrease their marketing costs–and decrease their number of sleepless nights worrying about the business, too.

Makes sense, right? Why spend resources trying to become known in a huge market when you can be perceived as the expert in your niche? Seth Godin calls it your "hive."[7] By focusing on your hive, your clients and customers will perceive more value in your services, and you'll see a greater return on your investment of time and money!

First, determine the life-time value of a customer or client. If you don't know the value of a customer in terms of actual dollars, how can you determine what you should spend in marketing to obtain that customer? Yet, I think 95% of businesses operate from some budget number based on a percentage of sales to determine what to spend on marketing this year. Calculating a lifetime value gives you a much better idea of what makes sense to spend.

Next, give the people you identify as potential hive members a *reason* to pay attention to you. Just like you, they have very busy lives; they're always looking for reasons *not* to pay attention. You need to provide something of value that will stop them long enough to hear that first message. It can be information or education or a free gift. If you're starting from scratch

---

[7]From the book *Permission Marketing*, by Seth Godin.

with no hive members, keep in mind, you'll have to offer *even greater* value or rewards!

- Determine the life-time value of a client.

- Focus—determine who is best served by your company. Don't try to be everything for everyone.

- Give them a reason to listen to you—to pay attention to you and your story.

- Understand this is an interactive process. Once and done on your part is not going to work.

- Build a relationship. Ask for continued permission to talk to them.

- Don't be a Luddite. Use the tools that are available today to communicate.

- Test, measure, test, measure.

- Be patient.

It's time to get back to basics. That's what professional football teams do every year at training camp. Start with determining the life-time customer value. You might be surprised at what you'll discover.

Ten Things to Do This Week

1. If you don't already know, determine the lifetime value of a client or customer to your company.

2. If you don't already know, determine how much it costs you to get a new client or customer.

3. Now that you do know, make sure you treat all your clients and customers with the value they deserve!

4. Send notes, photos, cards, and letters to your clients to thank them.

5. Create a newsletter (and/or blog) for your customers and clients.

6. Offer a "discount for prepayment" program.

7. Start a Frequent Buyer Program.

8. Survey your customers to see what you're doing right and what you can do better. Make it anonymous in order to get good data!

9. Make a note to learn all you can about your top 20 clients. Find out their hobbies, birth dates, family members names and interests, pets, etc. And, then communicate with them about all these things.

10. Send birthday cards, news clippings about their hobbies and interests, notes and postcards when you are traveling with information you know they will appreciate. Maybe it's your review of last night's meal or bottle of wine if you know they enjoy fine dining jotted on a postcard, or, try sending an autograph of their child's favorite sport star or news clipping on a topic of their interest.

You get the idea. If you don't, reread and implement numbers one and two!

Stop Marketing

Stop marketing your current products and services—at least, the way you're been marketing them for the past (insert number of years here).

Instead, create an extraordinary product or service that you can tell a fascinating story about—one that will excite people and make them want to be part of the story. If you keep telling people the same story and offering the same products and services, how can you expect things to change? You've got to tell a story *about change*—not about the status quo.

In a world where extraordinary, new, and exciting are demanded—status quo loses.

Listen First, and Tell Your Story

I've written about the importance of listening to your customers and prospects many times. I even created a selling system around it. The system focuses on finding out what your customers and prospects want and need. (It's called *Listen First–Sell Later.* Just like this book!)

But what if the customers don't really know what they want and need? What if they can't imagine the possibilities?

Henry Ford said that if he had asked prospects what they wanted when he was creating his vision of the automobile, they would have told him they wanted "a faster horse."

Politicians ask the voters what they want relative to the energy catastrophe and people say cheaper gasoline. They can't envision the possibilities. What if the politicians asked, "How would you like to have a Clean Energy System?" Thomas Friedman describes such a system in his book *Hot, Flat, and Crowded.*[8]

Roughly 40% of America's total CO_2 emissions come from the production of electricity used in homes, offices, and factories. Another 30% comes from cars, trucks, boats, trains and airplanes. Friedman states, "If we could electrify all of our transportation fleet, save for airplanes, and make all of them, and our buildings too, vastly more energy efficient at the same time—and then supply this whole 70%, buildings and transportation, with clean, abundant, cheap, reliable electrons through a smarter grid—that would be a revolution."

But right now people can't and won't answer the politicians' question like that. The idea is too abstract. They haven't been told the story of why they should want such a thing. They don't know that it's possible to create this system, right now, with American innovation. It doesn't matter that many of the pieces are ready to be put into place.

These people have been told too many stories of why they should continue the production of carbon dirty energy production, subsidized by our government and owned by petro-dictators. They are told these stories by *petro-dictatorships*, and energy companies who have a vested interest in keeping the current system. Those entities are doing a better job—at least in

[8]*Hot, Flat and Crowded* by Thomas Friedman is available on Amazon and from all major bookstores.

the US–of telling their story.

It's all about telling a story. You have a story, too. To be successful, you need to tell it. Don't wait for other people to tell it for you. Nobody tells it like you do. Don't let your competitors tell it–they'll be telling it with their own interests at heart.

Remember: In your story there will be one point you can't stress often enough. It will be the one thing that you want to make sure listeners take away with them. Do you know your "one thing?"

You only need a simple marketing plan and an even simpler business plan. Don't spend too much time on the name of your company, the logo design, the company mission statement or any of the other gobbledygook that the business books and schools obsess over.

You need your story. Start a fire with it. Burn your story into the hearts and minds of the people who want–who need–to hear it. They are out there waiting for you now.

What Story Is Your Business Card Telling?

I like having more than one business card design. I have a typical card, designed horizontally, with typical information (including phone, fax, address, logo, company tag line, email address and URL). These go to people who request it because they keep business cards in a standard file or system.

However, I also believe in being creative and getting your card noticed–so I like to use both sides of the card. Depending on your business, this is a place where you might put a visual or written display about you or your company. It's amazing how small you can make type that can be read. Have fun with this and tell a bit of your "story." Actually, just doing something fun and offbeat tells people some of your story!

I sometimes use humor on the back side of the business card. I've had cartoons made that make people smile. I've also printed some cards in full color, with a photo that I've created on both sides.

I also like designing vertical business cards. I've done vertical on one side and horizontal on the other to satisfy the personalities who like things all the same (horizontal) and those who like creativity (vertical).

If you happen to be exceptionally good looking, I'd recommend putting a professional photo of yourself on the card. Alas, you won't find any cards with my photo on them.

There's one other style of business card that I use: When people ask me for a business card, I reach into my pocket and pull out a 3.5 x 4 inch card printed on high quality paper using a photo printer. It always contains an image that I've created and some contact information. I put it together in Photoshop so I can print one at a time, and even customize it for events or different companies.

People enjoy the photos, and it's my belief that they hang on to them. I get their card at the same time. I follow up with a note telling them how I enjoyed meeting them, and I include one of my "normal" cards in the note. That gives me the opportunity to continue building the relationship.

Your business card actually can say a lot about you. What story does your card have to tell?

What Would Walter Cronkite Say?

I was watching a local network television channel yesterday evening when two things struck me as being "not right." I was viewing the local news in what is the third largest market in the country, when the newscaster segued from a story on child molestation to a new one telling me what the network would be telecasting later that evening during prime time. He made it sound like it was just another topical news story.

Now we all know this has been going on for a while–so I wasn't shocked. But I did experience two feelings, neither of them good. I felt sad for the veteran news anchor who probably never believed he would see the day when he'd be promoting the network entertainment as a news story. Can you imagine Walter Cronkite being told by network management that he has to tell the nation to tune in for The Biggest Loser or Big Brother 58? What do you think Walter would have told them?

The second feeling was one of being *mentally mugged* by the network. Networks have increased commercial time to over twenty minutes in one hour-long program. Now we even have to watch commercials in the actual programming, when a person who's supposed to be a news reporter becomes an advertising shill.

Big media thinks the answer to their declining market share is to interrupt us more and more. Many years ago my father predicted that network television would become nothing but commercials, and that you'd have to pay for each program you actually wanted to see without the commercials. I used to think he was just being a curmudgeon. Today, I realize he was prescient.

What Is That Advertising Really Costing You?

I see so much advertising in local papers and TV that I just don't understand how the results can be worth the cost to the advertisers. Most ads are "me too" ads that nobody pays any attention to these days. So why are we still spending so much money on this kind of advertising?

Today we are bombarded by ever increasing channels of communication. People change the channel when they're interrupted by your ad. Create a relationship with them; don't just tell them how you're better than the competition. Get their permission to maintain contact. Provide value that *they* value. Stop participating in an adult version of show and tell and *start asking questions*. Listen to them. Respect them.

It's a lot more work than telling your account rep to run that same ad again, but it will set you apart from 95% of the competition.

What's stopping you?

Advertising that Works for Better or Worse

I'm not a proponent of traditional media advertising by small businesses. Too many companies use it as a substitute for doing the hard work of marketing. They spend thousands (sometimes millions) of dollars on a few TV ads, and then complain that it didn't do much for them.

People talking are still the best form of advertising. Never forget that people will most readily believe what *other* people say about you, your company and your product or service.

I was in a wine store yesterday picking out a few bottles when I found a display of a Sauvignon Blanc that I think is excellent–especially for the price. All stores in Pennsylvania are run by the state and this particular store had never carried this wine. I was very pleased to see it, and I put several bottles in my cart. Then I noticed a woman standing next to me looking at white wines. I said hello and told her if she wanted to try a very good bottle she should buy this particular Sauvignon Blanc. I then described the wine to her. She said that she loved getting recommendations from people, and she bought a bottle of the wine I'd just recommended.

I've never seen this wine advertised in the media. I "discovered" it in Florida a couple of years ago when someone told me about it in a wine store. They said the same things I said yesterday. I bet the woman I told yesterday will be telling someone else after she enjoys the wine.

People are advertising for you every day. What you do as a company and as a business owner determines if they are selling for you or against you. Word-of-mouth is the most powerful advertising. What people say about you and your company can make or break your small business.

Great word-of-mouth *begins* with extraordinary products and services. It continues with extraordinary attention to your customers and your ability to exceed their expectations. And it's sustained by your passion for what you do.

How Do Customers Find You?

If you were a service company years ago, you could place an ad in the Yellow Pages and be pretty sure it would generate enough traffic to pay for the ad.

Today you need to have some of your potential customers' mind share *before* they need you. For example, let's say I'm thinking of three upcoming things I need to accomplish. I want to build an addition to my home, I have a big client party in mind for later in the year, and I'd like to find a good financial adviser. Since none of these things are immediately pressing (I don't have a roof leaking, for example), I have time to find various businesses to build, cater and advise. First I'd ask people whose judgment I trust for names of companies, because word of mouth is still the number one way of getting new business!

So how can word of mouth help your company get that mind share?

- You provide exceptional service and products so that people *want* to talk about you.

- You start today by asking your customers for permission to talk to them on a regular basis, and you collect their contact information.

- You start a blog that provides value and gives people a reason to use your services.

- You speak about your company and its services. (There are plenty of organizations who are looking for people to speak.)

- You make your customers feel special by providing them with a customer loyalty program that has real value (and also provides a reason to stay with your company).

- You make sure that the value of your service or product is far better than the cost.

That's a start (there are many more). What are you doing right now to make sure you're at the top of the list the next time someone asks a friend for the name of a ...?

Word of Bark Marketing

Many years ago when I lived in Pittsburgh, my girlfriend and I found a puppy that someone had abandoned. It was tiny and could fit in your hand. We tried to find the owner but apparently whoever had owned it didn't want it anymore. So "Sam" moved in with me and became my dog. He slept in my water bed the first night, found it suitable for his needs and slept there every night thereafter.

Shortly afterwards, I started getting requests from my girlfriend's twenty-year-old sons to borrow the dog to take to the local park. It seems that the easiest way to meet women, according to these two disreputable types, was to be seen walking a cute puppy. Women who otherwise would not give them a sideways glance would actually stop and engage them in conversation–and that often led to the exchange of phone numbers!

The girlfriend and Sam have been gone from my life for many years now, but my wife and I now have Max and Bucca–both Shih Tzu's just like Sam.

This brings me to a recent charity dog walk that was held in a large park near our home. Hundreds of dogs of all sizes and breeds converged on this park, towing their owners. It was quite a sight to behold! Max and Bucca could not have been happier–all those great smells spread out in a half mile in all directions! Bucca was a little overwhelmed with the sheer magnitude of it all, but Max has never been shy. Max greeted everyone (while posing for photos).

After about an hour of watching people watch the dogs, I experienced a flash back to when the guys used to borrow Sam back in Pittsburgh. Everywhere I turned there were a large number of single women walking their dogs. Single guys were making cooing noises as they showed their appreciation. Likewise, there were single guys with dogs who were searching for Ms. Right. But I thought at the time: The women have clearly gotten tired of being "manipulated by puppy" and have decided to take things into their own paws (so to speak).

Here's the marketing lesson. **Singles ads are advertising; puppy parks are word of mouth.** If you just walk a puppy in a park, you have a *fantastic* opportunity to meet more than one person, see them in a natural environment, have a reason to start a conversation, and still have plenty of time to decide if you'd like to meet again sometime (even if it is just to walk your dogs). The dog gives you permission to ask permission–"Oh, what a cute puppy. May I pet him?"

We can interrupt people all we want with ads, but there's nothing better than permission given by word of mouth when it comes to marketing.

Except maybe... word of bark.

If You Like Piña Coladas

Recently I happened to hear an old song that I think is called "The Piña Colada Song."[9] It's been stuck in my head for the past few days. However, it got me thinking about people who like piña coladas—and those that don't. I'm not a piña colada fan. I've been known to drink a Mai Tai when in Hawaii. But I find most sweet drinks—well, too sweet.

There must be plenty of people who *do* like piña coladas. As I thought about that, I started thinking about how some marketers waste time marketing piña coladas to people who *don't* like them (like me). We know that we don't like them, and it's unlikely that we're going to change our minds. It's pretty much wasted time and effort on anyone's part to try to change our minds.

If you're a piña colada marketer, you have a better option: Instead of trying to change our minds, why don't you spend that time and money to become the *best* piña colada maker in the world? Then, find (and focus your marketing efforts on) the people who are already predisposed to buy your drink. You can give them a way to tell all their friends (including other people with interest in piña coladas) about the best piña colada in the world—yours!

Apply this idea to whatever it is that you're marketing, and don't waste your time and money marketing stuff to people who don't want it. Find people who...

"Like Piña Coladas
Getting caught in the rain
And the feel of the ocean
And the taste of champagne"

[9]All you want to know about The Piña Colada Song:
http://en.wikipedia.org/wiki/Escape_(Rupert_Holmes_song)

I think you'll be happier with your marketing. And your customers will be happy you found them!

You've Got to Interrupt Them at Some Point

Having your clients' permission to communicate with them is your most important asset. In marketing, we call it permission marketing, or one-on-one marketing; marketing that is centered on a client's *consent* to market to them. Even viral marketing (which is a different animal) is sometimes called permission marketing.

However, it's important to understand that sooner or later (I'd suggest sooner), you need to tell that first person about what you do. You need to interrupt them.

Interruption marketing, which almost always must be used to get people interested in the first place, usually consists of unanticipated communications. But all interruption marketing is not a bad thing. When you consider that you have to get their attention at some point in order to get their permission, it becomes necessary. The key is to do that *without* turning them off to your message.

Here are some suggestions for creating the first interruption that allows you to bring value to the prospective client or customer.

1. Speak to them. Done well, speaking still attracts more people to respond to that first interruption than any other way for the small medium business person.

2. Write a book. Get it published traditionally if you can and if you have the time. If you don't have the time (it takes about a year for a publisher to get your book to market once you've written it), self publish it. This works exceptionally well if you also speak, have a defined niche or specialty, and want to use the book to market and make that first interruption.

3. Give the book to prospective clients. Interrupt them with it. You can ask for their email address in return. You can follow up with

more value–offer them your newsletter, let them know you speak; they may want you for their organization.

4. Give your current clients a discount if they buy the book for their employees. These employees move to other companies and will remember you if you have continued to add value to them with ongoing permission-based communication.

5. Write articles for newspapers, magazines, trade journals, and all their online iterations. It's easier to get published in most of the online versions.

6. Interview someone your prospective clients would like to hear (or have someone else interview them) and invite your clients to a free teleconference. Afterwards, post the digital file on your website. Blog and email it. Make sure it's not a commercial for you! If your clients need continuing education credits, get your presentations (both online and in-person) certified for CE's. Then use them to make that first interruption with the prospects.

7. Invite a select group of senior decision makers to an invitation only event where you and others will speak. Try beginning around 3:00 PM, last for 90 minutes, and follow it up with cocktails, light food and networking. I like having current clients there too–they'll often let prospective clients know they're working with you. And, they also get a chance to network.

8. Ask for referrals from your current clients. Ask them if they'd mind making an introduction, even if it's only an email introduction.

9. Sponsor a Speed Dating Business Development Meeting. Invite your current and prospective customers.

10. Invest in inbound marketing tactics such as blogging, RSS, free tools and trials, organic search engine optimization, social media, and public relations.

11. Whatever you do, once you make that first interruption and receive permission to communicate with the prospect, guard that

permission like your company's greatest asset. Permission builds trust and rapport and most people only buy from people they trust and like.

Killing the Goose

I've seen an uptick in the number of emails recently from companies who have my permission to email me. I'm a customer of three of them.

They used to email me about once a week with offers and promotions. Recently, two started emailing me almost daily and one finally went to multiple daily emails. Another went from bi-monthly announcements to two and three times a week.

Guess what–there was nothing new in any of the emails. Same products, same old story. I finally opted out of the one that sent me two and three emails a day. I can't see myself using their service again, as they never did anything to establish a relationship with me. I was just a goose they decided to kill with email saturation.

The other two companies are on the bubble. If they keep sending me more and more emails without telling me something new–without giving me a reason to read–I may be opting out of their lists, too.

Yes, the economy is hurting some of us. However, saying the same thing *more frequently* is going to backfire on you. The messages to be learned from the story of the goose who laid golden eggs are the following:

Gordon Gekko was wrong.[10]

Greed is not good. It destroys the source of good.

Actions like these may bring a quick return, but will ultimately lead to disaster.

Create a new story, new products, new services, and new reasons for someone to get excited about buying from you.

And take *really good* care of the geese.

[10]"Greed is Good" from the film Wall Street. http://en.wikipedia.org/wiki/Wall_Street_(film)

Goodbye Doesn't Have to Mean Forever

If you're using email with your customers, you of course must have their permission. (Otherwise it's called *spam*.) But do you also give them an easy way to unsubscribe?

People unsubscribe for a lot of reasons. Most are probably more emotional than rational. I get a lot of email for which I never gave permission—much of it happens when an organization I once belonged to sells or makes their members' email addresses available. I typically delete these messages after permanently blocking them. But one weekend, I decided to see how different companies deal with someone who unsubscribes.

The worst of the lot had a broken link when you hit unsubscribe. In other words, it didn't go anywhere. The largest companies told me it would take up to ten days to get me off their lists. (It should happen immediately.)

One person who bills himself as one of the nation's top marketers says you are instantly removed from the list, and then automatically redirects you to his web page where you can buy all his "stuff." He has continued to send me three emails a day every day since—so much for immediate removal!

Do you think because someone requests to be removed from a mailing list that they will never do business with you again? Why treat them with disrespect?

Treat your customers and readers like you would want to be treated. Goodbye doesn't have to mean forever.

It's Time for Permission Calling

After more than a decade of meetings and millions of dollars spent in research, legal fees, and more meetings, our political leaders have determined that most people don't want telephone calls made to their home without permission. They therefore created the National Do Not

Call Registry (NDNCR) in 2003, which is administered by the Federal Trade Commission.[11]

I find the NDNCR close to useless. My home phone still rings a half dozen times a day with calls from people who are exempt from it. Not counting Sundays, that means my home is getting over 1,800 unwanted phone calls a year.

The very first thing politicians did after making the law was to make exceptions. The first group they exempted was themselves. Yes, they determined that "we the people" really want to be called at home by politicians and their representatives–even if it's for the purpose of asking for money. Next they added charities. I assume in their minds this was some sort of political slime offset (not unlike a carbon offset).

Additionally, they exempted:

- People or companies conducting surveys.

- Companies with which you have an existing business relationship, up to 18 months after your last purchase, payment, or delivery from that company. (Think about this the next time a store asks you for your phone number when you check out. By purchasing from them you are now subject to telemarketing from them for the next year and a half.)

- Companies can also call you up to three months after you submit an inquiry to that company. That's right–call for some information and you're fair game unless you *specifically* tell them not to contact you.

- There's also a loophole that allows mortgage companies to call you with unsolicited offers if you've applied for a mortgage. The FTC identifies this as a pre-screened offer, which is allowed. You can't make this stuff up.

It was recently election season here in the United States, which means we were being bombarded by political calls. In my case, 100% of them came from automatic robot dialers with a recorded message. It makes you want to avoid voting for the person calling (though if we followed that rule, there would be nobody at the polls on Election Day).

[11]The Federal Trade Commission and the National Do Not Call Registry: https://www.donotcall.gov/

Even if you check Caller ID, most of the callers block their true identity and numbers. Even with Caller ID, your phone is still ringing all the time with calls from people who do not have your permission to call.

I could go on with the exceptions, exemptions and Catch 22 rules, but the fact is that the Do Not Call Registry does not work. With that in mind, I think it's time to start a "Permission Calling Initiative." It's a simple concept.

- First, you register the phone numbers of people from whom you wish to get phone calls. The registry doesn't have to be a government entity. We can get rid of the department at the FTC that's administering the list and use the money saved to help bail out one of those mortgage companies that was making too many "pre-screened offers." It could be done with your own phone and some additional technical features in the equipment.

- If someone calls you who isn't on your "call registry" they need to have their Caller ID unblocked. That way you can look at your Caller ID and see if you want to take a call. Anyone whose ID is blocked won't be able to ring your number, and you can choose whether their call will automatically go to your voice mail, or if they'll hear a message telling them to unblock their number.

- If you get a call from a number and it isn't someone you want to hear from again, you simply enter a code on the keypad and they're blocked from even being able to ring your phone.

- There are no exceptions, except for emergency and law enforcement personnel.

Is this all a pipe dream? Of course it is—if we wait for our government to implement it. They have too many vested interests to do what's right. We don't need our political leaders' permission to do this. We don't need to ask the FTC if it's okay with them. We just need someone tinkering in their garage to invent the technology so we can implement it ourselves in our own homes. In fact, some of this technology already exists. I think it should be part of every phone sold. We shouldn't even have to buy an add-on service or piece of equipment.

Until that happens–keep tinkering.

Imagine what a feature like this could mean in terms of permission. How many telephones are there in the US? In the world? People are bombarded with interruption marketing. It's why permission marketing works. It's why you'll see more and more technical solutions on the personal level to help stop the interruptions.

How to Sell Pizza (or Anything Else)

If you're opening a small business in a down economy or during boom times, you need to think a few things through before you open your doors for business.

A pizzeria-style Italian restaurant recently opened in my area. I wouldn't have known it, but they had someone stuff a menu in our door. It was a menu just like every other pizzeria menu. It didn't give me a reason to visit them. They have the same specials as all the pizzerias. The menu is printed on stock paper with stock photos that lots of restaurants use. There is nothing in their first contact with me (a potential customer) that makes me want to give them a try.

As I looked the menu over, I noticed that I didn't see anything about delivery service. Pretty much all the pizza places here deliver. The ones that don't just threw away at least half of their business.

Then I noticed one of their coupons, which stated "Good only for dining in or take out." Logic told me that if it's only good for those two things, they must have another service where it *isn't* good–and the only one that made sense was delivery. So, I called them and asked.

"No, we don't deliver," they said.

I said, "I'm confused–your menu offers discounts only on dining in your restaurant or taking food out. How would I buy your product in a situation where I couldn't use the coupon?"

"We don't deliver," was the response, and that was the end of the conversation.

Here's what I would have done if I was opening a new pizzeria-style Italian restaurant and planning to deliver flyers to potential customers:

1. I would have the best pizza in town.

2. The flyer would be an offer of a free pizza. (I'd spread the flyers out over a couple of weeks.)

3. I'd have free delivery, and I'd make sure I paid the delivery people well to give the best possible service.

4. I would have my delivery people wear costumes. We'd change them from time-to-time. Imagine if the pizza was delivered by someone dressed as a gorilla.

5. Every time someone got home delivery or bought at my restaurant, I'd include a little something extra they weren't expecting.

6. When they'd come into the restaurant to eat, the server would give them a free pizza coupon at the end of their meal. They would also be handed a postcard and a pen with an offer to give a friend a free pizza too. We then would take the card and put it in the mail for them.

7. We'd have a birthday club. Members would get a birthday card and coupon for a free dinner at the restaurant anytime during their birthday week.

I wouldn't do what every other pizza place does. I'd make it a fun experience whether customers were coming into the restaurant or calling for delivery.

With a little creativity, you can substitute pretty much any other product or service for the pizza, like software or employment services.

Creativity Just Is

Some people think they aren't creative. They are correct.

Some people who experience creativity believe they *are* creative. They are incorrect.

Inherently, people are neither creative nor uncreative.

Creativity *is*. By that I mean it already exists. All ideas exist but just haven't been revealed. If you believe this to be true then everyone can engage in the process of creativity.

All of us know how to engage in the creative process from the time we are babies. We grow in the process until our structured school systems beat it out of us (unless we're lucky). When I was in second grade I got an "F" in art because I didn't like the things they gave me to color–so I created my own picture by enhancing and changing what I was given. I've never been very good at staying between the lines.

I believed I was an art failure and had no creativity until I happily experienced the process of developing photographs in the darkroom at the age of 13. I jumped into photography. I didn't care about "not being creative." I was caught up in something magical. I went on to become a national award winning photographer and a professional photojournalist for many years. I still do it to engage in an alternative creative process.[12]

I tell you this story because I want you to believe, as I do, that the creativity was always there. The works of art always existed. I believed I could manifest them, and they became real. Each one of us can do the same thing.

This means there is *no reason* to accept that you can't change things for the better, regardless of the specific application or circumstances. There is *no reason* not to engage in the process of manifesting creativity to make a positive change to your life, your job, or your business.

The process of creativity is enormously gratifying and uplifting for both body and soul. It becomes exponentially more so when you engage in the process with other like-minded people. Get together with some friends, co-workers, or employees. Do some creativity exercises to get your mind flowing. Perhaps you can use mind mapping.[13] Let yourself focus on

[12]My photography is online here: http://bobpoole.com/
[13]Mind mapping: http://en.wikipedia.org/wiki/Mind_map

thinking of ideas. No idea is too far out! None is discarded, because that idea may lead to *the one* that changes everything for you.

Start with one problem, one challenge for which you'd like to find a really creative solution. Perhaps it could be, "How do we take advantage of a down economy?" That might be a good start for many of us. Depending on when you read this book, it might be another!

Right now as I write this, I'm engaging in an all day exercise led by Steven Robbins with about a dozen other people who are supporting each other in getting stuff done.[14] We started the day by stating our goals. Then we stated an hourly goal and we check in and support each other every hour. It's working. People are getting more done than ever by using the collective power of the group. You can apply this concept to your own creativity, and help others at the same time.

Engage in the creative process. You'll find the journey very satisfying, and I'll wager you'll end up in a place of contentment–a place where creativity is.

Become a Kid Again

My grandson, Michael, is two years old and very creative. I bet your children and grandchildren are very creative too. Too many of us lose this by the time we're adults.

To a two-year-old everything is new and creates a sense of wonder. He doesn't have any preconceptions about what something should look like. An elephant can be pink and the ocean can be purple. A two-year-old sees in different ways than we do when we get older.

Creativity is necessary in your business and sales career. Too many people become specialists in their products and services and lose the balance that creativity could bring to their lives. I've made it a point my entire life to learn as much as I can about anything. You need to re-learn how to see in different ways, if you're not already doing it.

You can't be an artist and ignore technology. You can't be an accountant and ignore the arts. We are all connected to each other; to ignore

---

[14]Steven Robbins is the Get-It-Done Guy™: http://getitdone.quickanddirtytips.com/

learning, experiencing, and creating is to risk becoming stagnant and one dimensional.

Become a kid again. Go to the bookstore and buy a book you'd never read. If all you read is non-fiction, buy a fictional story–and vice-versa.

Pick it because you like the title or the cover.

Let it inspire you.

Do You Have a Monkey Mind?

I often lie in bed at night right before I go to sleep experiencing what I call Monkey Mind. Notice I don't say that I'm suffering from it. Monkey Mind to me is that time when you're all alone with your thoughts about your business or clients or the sales call you have planned tomorrow. Your mind tends to race from one thought to another like a monkey jumps from tree to tree. This kind of thinking would be distracting much of the time and there are therapists who work to eliminate these thoughts, but I find it also can be very creative.

I suspect most business owners sometimes find themselves awake at night thinking about the company. It's stressful running a company and there are things that keep our minds whirling. But try turning it into a positive experience: I let my mind jump around and, if you can imagine doing this, I stand back and watch it as an observer. When it jumps to a thought that seems interesting to me–the observer–I engage myself fully in the process. That's when I get some of my better ideas!

Keep a digital recorder or lighted pen and paper next to the bed. Write your ideas down immediately. If you don't, you'll often realize they were fleeting–and then they're gone.

In the morning take a look at the list or listen to the recording over your breakfast. Often what seemed like a good idea turns out to be one the monkey should have kept. But just as often, you may find the solution for a problem, an insight into someone who works for you, or a creative marketing idea that you can implement today.

When you're ready to sleep, become the observer again and say good night to the monkey. Let the thoughts rise and float away into the trees. If you still need help sleeping, try a glass of warm milk blended with a banana.

Some Things I Wonder About

I have always been a proponent of companies and salespeople sending birthday cards to their customers. It's a great way to connect, an opportunity to be creative, and both those things are essential to building a positive customer relationship. But now I wonder–maybe it's a better idea to give the customer a phone call. Communication is getting more impersonal, and I wonder if a phone call would mean more to them. What do you think?

I've read that 70% of communication is non-verbal. I wonder who comes up with these numbers. Are they real or do they become "real" because they get repeated so many times?

A sales expert is espousing that numbers don't work anymore when it comes to making sales calls. She says you can actually do more harm by making more calls. That might be true if you're totally inept, but you can take this to the bank: Work harder, make more calls and you'll make more sales. (Where do they come up with this stuff?)

This same sales expert also says it takes at least 10 contacts before you make a sale. Wow. I don't know how to break this to the thousands of salespeople who are out there making sales in one call. I wonder what I'm supposed to do the next time someone indicates they want to buy from me and we've only had two contacts?

I recently read about how the Human Resource department of a multi-billion dollar software company hired a sales assessment company to create a hiring profile for hiring successful salespeople. They determined there are 80–yes, that's 80–key indicators of successful salespeople in this particular company. I wonder how they apply that to hiring their salespeople. I wonder if that means you don't have to interview or even meet candidates anymore!

How do you screen for 80 key indicators? I think five is plenty, and you're lucky if you can determine all of them. I guess with this profile you could do all your screening over the internet, just using the assessment profile. Think of the time and money savings! What I really wonder is, who's the idiot that allowed Human Resources to have anything to do with hiring salespeople?

I have a client who finds people jobs–both permanent and temporary– in a licensed professional field. He sends out weekly job bulletins, information about Continuing Education workshops, and a monthly educational newsletter. I have always wondered why a person who asks to be on their 100% permission-based mailing list later takes themselves off permanently, when they get a job. Don't they want to know what's going on in their field? Do they think they'll work for one company forever? I've always wondered what goes through their minds.

I wonder why more people don't expect the best to happen (instead of the worst)? Why do they allow themselves to be paralyzed by fear? People who need to know something is perfectly safe before trying it never get anywhere. Remember Indiana Jones and the Holy Grail?[15] The final step was a "Leap of Faith." You have to have faith the best will happen. You have to know it won't always work out, too–and you have to pick yourself up and try again.

I wonder why some people treat waiters, dry cleaners, the train conductor and the checkout clerk so poorly. Are they only nice to the people they think are like them? Why can't they even make eye contact with those people?

I wonder why some people are always chasing after the cheapest price, even if it means giving up a relationship. Don't they know that a quality life is all about relationships?

Relationships Work

When you're considering the effect of great relationships on your business, don't overlook the business relationships! One of the most over-

---

[15]Indiana Jones and the Last Crusade: http://www.imdb.com/title/tt0097576/

looked (and most effective) marketing tactics is to team up with another company, yet relatively few companies actually do it. I'm not sure why. It takes work and a good value proposition to convince another company to market your product or service, but I don't think that's the real reason. I think a lot of companies are afraid of letting someone else "touch their stuff." Silly–I know.

Here's a real life example of how it might work:

My client was one of the top ten companies in home security. They did most of their expansion through expensive telemarketing and direct sales. I proposed that we approach companies with very large pre-existing customer bases and offer them the opportunity to market the security system as added value. Some were utility companies; one was a very large automobile club. Several loved the idea.

My client got increased sales of their security systems. Our partner companies got increased revenue in the way of a commission, and they were viewed by their customers as offering an added value. And we offered the consumer a discount on the system as the added benefit!

It was a win–win–win relationship.

Turn It into a Fund Raiser

How do you get free media coverage for your company while having other people sell your products or services? You might think about doing what a health club I worked with did one year.

Every year this health club would conduct a big membership campaign. They always bought radio commercials and placed print ads in the local newspapers. They also had to pay their staff extra for all the hours they needed to staff for walk-ins and appointments. They got about the same number of new members every year. It worked for them, but they were looking for another way. We decided to turn their membership campaign into a fund raiser!

Here's a thumbnail sketch of the idea and the process:

1. The health club previously charged an initiation fee of $100 (which was really part of the staff's compensation)–and we decided to give that $100 away.

2. We learned that the most active civic organization in town was a group that raised money for college scholarships. Their primary fund raising method was a hoagie sandwich sale they conducted a few times a year.

3. We learned from them that if we gave them the $100 from each new membership, they could easily make ten times as much as they made on hoagies.

4. We offered them the $100 initiation fee if they would staff the club and sell the memberships for the campaign. They accepted. We now had a sales force of over 150 people!

5. We helped them contact the local media with the news that they were conducting a fund raiser in conjunction with the health club to give away scholarships. The media loved the story and we got lots of free coverage, including television. They even followed the campaign with updates on its progress.

6. The service organization sold *four times* the usual number of memberships. (Plus, many of them also joined the health club as first time members.)

7. My client's club got more members than ever at a lower cost per member, and was viewed by the public as doing something great for the community. The service organization made more money for scholarships than they ever had, with less work. And more kids got college scholarship money!

Once again, it was a triple-win marketing program! You can do the same thing with a little creative thinking.

Things to Do in the Next 12 Months

- Write your manifesto. Blog it. Put it in your newsletter. (Live it.)

- Create a presentation in order to support and carry out your manifesto. Make sure whoever sits and listens to the presentation comes away feeling like it was a good investment of their time. Create value for them, and leave them with information they'll use and pass on to others.

- Make a list of everyone who'd be willing to listen to your presentation. Send them a letter with compelling reasons for them to accept your presentation offer. Start booking dates.

- Risk being vulnerable as you share your message.

- Put together an eBook and make it available for free on-line. It will tie in with your manifesto.

- Write a book (you're ready–you've been ready) and self-publish it with Lulu[16] (or any number of companies). Decide if you will sell it or give it away.

- Collaborate with people like yourself, and with people totally different than yourself. Create something special that makes a difference in your world.

- Learn something new–something you've always wanted to do. Then teach it to someone else!

- Write a letter to someone who changed your life for the better. It could be a teacher, a friend, or anyone who made a difference. Give them the letter. Don't wait until it's too late. Eulogies are highly overrated.

- Embrace failure. Without it, you aren't really trying.

- Try to start each day by remembering that we're all connected. I have faith that if each of us remembers, it could make a world of difference.

---

[16]This book was published using Lightning Source: http://www.lightningsource.com/

How to Get Rid of Your Office Cost

Twenty years ago I thought it was important to have an office. Even though I'd worked alone for many years, I thought that clients wouldn't take me seriously without an office outside my home. In the early 1990s a company that wanted to form a contractual relationship with me (with whom I had worked for almost a year), wanted to see my office as the final step before signing off. I went along with it at the time, but today I wonder if they'd still need to see a "real office."

Two decades have passed since then, and it appears that most companies still think it's necessary to have their employees "come to the office" everyday. Are they fearful that allowing people to work from home would decrease the quality and quantity of their work? All the studies I've seen over the last twenty years state just the opposite. Not only is the work just as good, but the employees are happier!

What are some reasons you should consider getting rid of the office?

- Think of the money you'll save on a brick and mortar building, and all its associated costs.

- The average employee will get an instant pay raise, since she won't have to pay for transportation.

- You'll be doing the environment a favor, and helping to break the bonds with petro-dictators.

- You can hire talented people anywhere in the country and you won't have to move them to you.

- Employees love flexibility and will therefore be happier and more productive.

- It stops turnover due to spouse/partner issues—for instance, if one is offered a new job in another location.

- You can be more flexible in staffing hours, and offer increased service to customers before or beyond your normal working hours.

Are Trade Shows Worth the Investment?

When it comes to B-to-B marketing, trade show revenue surpassed print revenue for the first time in 2006 (according to American Business Media[17]). Many small business owners tell me they have a difficult time justifying the investment in exhibiting at trade shows. Let's face it–trade shows are expensive and time consuming. But if you're going to make the investment, why not get the best results you can–and track them?

Trade shows provide you with lots of potential and current clients all in one place at one time. Visitors are there to shop, compare, be educated and listen to your story. They go to make decisions on buying products and services.

Here are some things you can do to get a return on your trade show investment:

- Volunteer to speak. Trade shows are always accompanied by a host of presentations. Put together an educational story that will add value to the lives and businesses of the people who attend. You'll gain enormous credibility. Let people who visit your booth know that you're speaking.

- Send out a mailing to your clients who are attending. Let them know about your presentation. Host an invitation-only party in your hotel suite for top clients and prospects. Let your clients tell your story! Remember, people are most likely to believe what *others* say about you and your company.

- Get free PR and media exposure–local press and trade press cover the large shows. Make sure you send them mail before the show. Offer to be a resource.

- Collect leads! Here is where strange things start happening for small companies. I've seen too many people working a booth at a trade show collect a business card, then write a note on it and put it in their pocket. **Cards get lost.** What you wrote today becomes a code you can't break when you get home. When you meet people at a trade show, get their permission to follow up with information about your

[17]American Business Media: http://www.americanbusinessmedia.com/

company, products and services. Enter them into your database immediately. Invest in the card reader many shows offer today which puts everyone into a database. If you have a sales team there, *do not* let the salespeople collect the cards. Bring a detail-minded administrative person whose sole job it is to collect and control contact information and requests.

- Follow-up immediately after the show is over. Thank your contacts for stopping to see you and give them the information you promised. Continue to slowly build the relationship you started at the show. I would bet that at least 80% of leads generated at a trade show *do not* get followed-up correctly–or at all. What a waste!

- Depending on your business, you can sell at a trade show. Some shows don't allow you to deliver products on the spot, but you can still take orders. You can offer a show special that's only available at the show.

- Network with everyone, including your competition. Attend the social functions. Don't hide in your room at the end of the exhibition hours. Be visible.

- Pick an evening and take a few of your top clients to dinner.

- There are lots of other things you can do, depending on your type of business. You might want to look for distributors for your product. Perhaps you're ready to add to your sales force; you can meet lots of salespeople at trade shows. You can set up meetings with your customers and business partners. You can save lots of money and time by conducting meetings at these kinds of events. (Don't do it on the trade show floor, though. I always get a suite with a room that I can set up for meetings.)

- If you have a new company, want to make a big impression and want to establish your company as a player in the industry–go big. Here's what I mean: Invest in as much space as possible, create a fantastic display, do a pre-trade show mailing and hire someone like Paul Gertner to attract people to your area.[18]

[18]Paul Gertner is one of the world's greatest magicians, and his website is here: http://www.gertner.com/

When I started a highly specialized software company in the early '90s, I knew I was up against some big companies. But I also knew we had a unique story that should be very attractive to our prospective base. The industry had one major national convention and trade show every year. I decided to launch the company at that show, with the biggest exhibit we could afford (and with the help of Paul Gertner!). We made a big impression, we were the talk of the show, and immediately established ourselves as a force in the market. We followed up the next year with an even larger exhibit and Paul's help again.

Trade shows should not be an expense–they should be an investment. They can be an excellent investment, but make sure to employ ideas that get a trackable return. Otherwise, why be there at all?

Dumb Marketing

If you live on the East Coast, you're probably very familiar with Commerce Bank and their ubiquitous red logo–"Mr. C." I can't imagine that any other regional bank has spent more money over the years building their brand. (For a couple of years now, they've been using Regis and Kelly as spokespeople.)

Commerce has now merged with TD Banknorth. If that name doesn't jump out at you, I wouldn't be surprised. They're based in Toronto, Canada and they aren't a household name.

However, TD Banknorth has decided that the Big Red C millions of people recognize has to go. They've replaced it with a green TD logo that has "Commerce Bank" written in plain black lettering to one side.

I'm sure TD must have a good reason for getting rid of the one bank logo that millions of people recognize and creating a new one. Maybe they had millions of dollars they needed to spend on new signage, printing, and everything else they got with the Commerce acquisition that had to do with marketing.

I would have kept the Big Red C. Customers have gone through too many bank mergers over the years (especially ones that are examples of the worst customer service transitions on record) to have one more "new thing" thrown at them at this time. Commerce is known by its customers as having great customer service. Why call attention to the fact that the bank you love is no longer the same bank?

From the "You Really Can't Make This Stuff Up" files: There's a quote in the March 28th, 2008 Philadelphia Business Journal from a TD Banknorth spokesperson in response to criticism about the change: "From our research, customers told us that names and logos are not as important as service."

Of course names and logos aren't as important as service. But before you've proven your customer service in a transition, there's a good chance you'll lose trusting customers solely on the basis that they don't yet know or trust you (even if they knew and trusted the company you're merging with). Changing an identity that holds positive meaning for the people you want to serve changes your ability to interact with them.

I hope they didn't pay too much for that research.

Quickly Increase Business Income

Here's a list of things you can do right now to quickly increase your business income. How many of them can you accomplish this month?

- Cut out the lowest profit, time, or resource consuming activities. Invest more in the highest pay-off activities. I know owners who love to spend time on the computer browsing the web for information when they could be talking to their best customers and prospects instead.

- Increase the frequency with which your clients purchase your products and services. In other words, increase repeat business. Give them a reason to buy again soon. Follow up with every customer who buys from you–and every one that doesn't. This doesn't have to be used only in B-to-C but can also be used successfully in B-to-B sales.

- Raise your fees or prices without sacrificing sales volumes. You should be raising prices a little bit on a regular basis. People hate being hit with a big price raise even if you haven't raised them in years. Better to do it regularly.

- Increase your number of clients—preferably with little cost to you. Get referrals, write articles, speak, network, volunteer for boards, do some pro bono work, and give back to your community.

- Propose an "Up-selling Offer" in every transaction. Ever notice when you buy a man's suit that the salesperson will always up-sell you to two suits—for a much better price per unit? Plus there are shirts, ties, and other accessories. Apply the same concept to your business.

- Create a paid membership club. It's a lot easier and more cost effective to sell to people who are already aware of your products and services, than to find new customers. Your current customers already like and trust you. Reward them with a good deal for being a member of your club. It gives you regular, predictable income and creates a sense of family and community.

- License or franchise your products or services. (I like licensing.) You've got a great idea that you use in your geography; why not find other companies like yours who would pay a license fee for the materials, marketing, and methodologies in order to increase their own income?

- Create relationships with other companies where they sell you products or services, and vice versa.

- Start an affiliate program. This is different than the relationship program, which is more symbiotic in nature. An affiliate usually has their own business and wishes to add to their own product or service line without adding costs like development or inventory. Basically, they act as a representative for your company.

- Increase your operational efficiencies. However, don't fire the person who answers the phone unless its desperation time. Better to use the other nine ideas first than for you, the owner, to be spending time doing tasks you can have someone else do at a better cost. What is your time worth?

The Single Most Important Thing You Can Do Now to Increase Business!

When the economy is difficult, the media just can't talk enough about it. Sometimes I wonder if they're getting paid by the number of times they mention it in one day. Regardless, it can lead to thoughts about how business will fare in tough times.

How would you actually like to grow and prosper? Here is the *single most important thing* you can do for your small business right now:

Get out and speak!

Speak about your services or products. Don't make it a commercial. (Nobody wants to hear that.) Tell people how their lives or businesses can be improved. Focus on providing them value so that they leave feeling like they made a great investment of their time in listening to you.

Speaking will position you as the expert in your personal hive. Make it interesting! Join Toastmasters[19] if you need help in preparing and learning how to speak–or get a referral to a good speaking coach in your community.

Do it now. Your competition won't do it. You'll end up seeing growth now *and* in the future.

Chicken, Ribs, and Exponential Growth

Last year I helped one friend put on a summer celebration for a hundred people on his farm. This past Saturday night, another friend hosted a party for five hundred people. The smaller event worried my first friend because they'd never hosted a party for that many people at

---

[19] Toastmasters International: http://www.toastmasters.org/

once. However, my friend who hosted the larger party was unfazed. Why? Because in the past, he's been involved for years in hosting the largest high school alumni association celebration in the country–thousands attend. They typically break records for the amount of chicken and ribs served at their sit down barbecue dinner.

That got me to thinking about business owners and salespeople. Typically sometime in December, we sit down and plan for the coming year. We set goals, and salespeople are given quotas. Both are usually no more than a 20% increase, and many people just hope to be able to do as well as they did the past year.

But, what stops us from doing even more? What holds us back from exponential growth? Most often, the thing that holds is back is a *belief* that it can't be done. A salesperson will say, "I worked liked crazy this year; there's no way I can increase sales more than 10% next year." Likewise, the business owner tells himself that he can't work any more hours, and hopes for a good year.

What do you think would happen if you actually *did* have a fantastic year? Let's say you increased sales by 50%. You'd no longer be able to walk around believing it can't be done. And you could do it again! I know that for a fact because I've done it, and I've seen it done by many others. So what's holding you back from doing it now? Stop thinking about the economy, and believe.

By the way–contrary to some pop psychology, you can't just think about it in order for it to happen. You still have to *do the work*; you still have to grill the chicken and cook the ribs.

But serving chicken and ribs to five hundred people is a walk in the park when you've already served thousands!

We Don't Need Business Ethics

Have you ever heard someone apologize and say something like "Don't take it personally, it's only business?" I've heard it. And, as my father would have said, "It's a bunch of hooey."

A friend of mine has three rules for life. They are:

- **Do what's right.**
- **Do your best.**
- **Treat others as you would like to be treated.**[20]

You have a life. It includes everything, including business. You have no authorization to treat people any differently in business than you would treat someone you love. To do so is self-demeaning and usually used as an excuse for greed and the pursuit of materialism above doing what's right.

Nowhere in these rules does it say that there's one set of guiding principles for your personal life and another set for your business life. The idea that a different set of rules governs business (and you as a business person) is how economies get into messes (like the one it's in as I write this). Companies don't need a set of business ethics. They need to operate by a set of *human ethics*.

It's up to all of us to **stop making excuses** for a different set of rules for business.

Profits Are Not Just Money

Being in business or starting a business to make money is a difficult way to live. Don't get me wrong–profit is the reason a business exists. But to "do" a business with only the profit motive is no better than spending your life as a corporate drone in a cubicle wishing and saying "if only."

Profits are not only money. Profit is what I get as your customer, your employee or your supplier. A business must contribute some kind of profit to all that it touches or it will not–it *cannot* be successful. A business simply can't be successful at the expense of others. It may put money into pockets, but it can't be thought of as successful if others suffer or lose as a result.

If you are in business (or in a job) where your only profit is money, you are *not* in the right place. Would you sell your soul for money? Business and life are not separate things. You cannot be in

[20]You can find more quotes from Lou Holtz here:
http://www.brainyquote.com/quotes/authors/l/lou_holtz.html

business and compartmentalize it from the rest of your life. You cannot compartmentalize it from your soul.

Be in business because you love what you're doing–because you love helping everyone in and around your business to profit. The "profits" will be that much greater.

And the journey will be so much more interesting.

Better Than Anyone

Do you value your employees?

I'd wager you answered "yes" to that question. But do you really? Do you take care of them better than anybody else can?

You might believe you do, but if you can't spell out how you do it, you may have a problem–or maybe you're a business owner who doesn't believe you *need* to take care of them better than anyone else can. If that's the case, read no further. You're in the wrong line of work.

I've had business people tell me that they can easily replace employees during rough economic times, since the available pool is larger. With that kind of employer attitude, my guess is that they really aren't taking care of their current employees better than anyone else. Treating employees like commodities when times are rough will come back to bite you, well, "you know where"–and when things get better, your best people will leave.

Let your employees know they are valued, and that you care about them personally. If you aren't a "people person" and aren't capable of being empathic, then I'd suggest you get a partner or someone who is capable. Listen to them. Ask them their advice. Allow them to put themselves in your shoes. Let them know you heard them, and give them feedback.

If you need one last reason to take care of your employees better, remember this: If you do, odds are that your employees will be taking care of your customers the same way–better than anyone else can.

It Has Nothing to Do With Paper Towels

Too many business owners focus on things *within* their company. The worst have taught their employees not to make a decision without involving them. I saw one business owner take one of his staff to task over the kind of paper towels they were using in the company kitchen. Another berated his number one employee (his son) over the placement of a merchandising rack. He then moved it about six inches–and said it was perfect.

If you see yourself in the paragraph above, you really need to stop it!

Focus *outside* the organization. Let your subordinates make decisions and make mistakes. Let them learn from them. You need to be looking at how best to provide value for your clients and your company.

Believe me–it's not by choosing paper towels.

Sales Is a Lonely Job

If you've been a professional salesperson, you know that outside sales is a lonely job with lots of rejection. Salespeople need to be in each other's company for support, and they need to see their managers even more so for the same reasons. This is a wonderful way to take care of your employees and ensure that they feel valued in your organization. They need to know they aren't alone out there. Meetings give them a chance to talk and learn from each other, and they undoubtedly learn best in a face-to-face setting. It's important to have regional and annual meetings for those reasons–not to mention that they allow you to bring in great speakers and have lots of social networking.

Virtual meetings are just plain boring, especially with (or despite) technological problems. With virtual meetings you don't get instant feedback, which is something both salespeople and sales management need in order to be effective.

An in-person meeting with speakers who can add value to your employees' sales and marketing process can say a lot about the culture of the company and set expectations. You can't do that in a virtual meeting.

Remember, too, that while in-person meetings instill in your salespeople the belief that they're important to the company, take the meetings away and the belief goes too. That's why C-Level attendance–CEO, CFO, CTO, CMO–should always be mandatory. I've seen employees watch extremely important video and virtual presentations by the CEO, presentations that would affect their future. What I see in their eyes, though, is "we're not important enough for you to actually be here." It's even worse when they know she's sitting in her office on the top floor.

Connect your salespeople to each other, but let them connect to *you* as well.

Trust Not Tools

There seems to be a major push right now for sales productivity tools. They're being foisted on salespeople to solve problems in a difficult economy. I just have to be a contrarian and say, enough is enough!

Customer Relationship Management, time tools, sales process and performance solutions, sales analytics, and a host of other tools that claim to get you more leads, manage your time, let you forecast, direct you to the "right" customer, or, the one I really like, "**exploit** your customer relationships," are all for sale.

I've been a sales and marketing professional since the 1960s. I've seen every tool come and go. The one thing that every single one of them has in common is this: Professional salespeople hate them, and won't use them.

I've seen CRM tools that take a week of class time to begin to learn and then a few more hours out of your sales and marketing time to use them. Who buys these things? My sense is that it's usually analytical management types who want to get "their arms around sales." These people often have never really sold for a living, and they don't feel at all comfortable with the squishiness of sales numbers and the sales process. So they buy a tool they think will give them the data they need to do their job, and then they force it on their salespeople as well.

If you force people to use tools like these, they'll fudge the numbers.

You'll never get the data you want, and you just might lose the best and brightest in your sales force. They won't use something that won't help them in their job–and they sure won't use it if it hurts them.

Here's an idea for sales and marketing VPs, and managers:

- Get out of the office and spend time with your salespeople. (And not just once a quarter, or once a year!)

- Ask the best ones what they need to do a better job. Really listen to what they say.

- Go on sales calls and listen with your eyes, ears, and heart open (and your mouth shut).

Learn to trust your sales force, and you won't have nearly as much need to "get your arms around them"–except to *thank them* for their efforts and achievements. If they actually need tools to do their jobs better, they will tell you. They will ask you for them!

It's about trust–not tools.

Why Do Large Companies Spend Too Much On Sales Training?

Why is it that when it comes to implementing a sales training program, large companies almost always go with the most expensive, most complicated, and least effective?

I have evaluated many, many programs. The worst ones were always so complicated to understand and implement that I knew the program would be abandoned by most sales teams within 60 days after being launched. Those that weren't abandoned were kept alive because the VP of sales was the person who made the decision to use it. Until he was gone, all hope of a program that worked was gone, too.

The absolute best sales training program I ever saw was one created by Ron Willingham in the eighties.[21] He originally called it *The Best Seller* and he wrote a book by the same title. (He later wrote another called *Integrity Selling for the 21st Century*.)

---

[21] *The Best Seller* by Ron Willingham can be bought used on Amazon.

Why was it so good? Because it was simple, it was based on principles and not techniques, and it wasn't manipulative in any way. Even if you weren't a salesperson, you could read it and become successful. If you'd been selling for many years, reading it would get you back to basics and increase your sales.

All the training materials were around fifty dollars a person. Pay for a facilitator, and you had a program that increased sales exponentially. I never saw it fail to get excellent results.

The last program I evaluated cost six figures and was considered a joke in the sales force of the large company that was implementing it. I never saw it used past the classroom. Large companies fall into a trap of believing that if a program has lots of bells and whistles and costs a lot, it must be really good. They need to see lots of "stuff" in order to justify the big price tag. The people who buy these kinds of programs have a belief that sales strategies need to be complex–which is totally wrong.

Small companies can't afford these kinds of programs (or mistakes). In fact, most of the big name training companies will ignore you if you're small. If you're looking for a sales program, though, there are lots of good independent people who can help you. Look for someone who has actually sold and been successful.

Higher price and complexity does not necessarily equate to higher quality and results when it comes to sales training.

Sales Isn't a Four Letter Word

Many years ago when I first started teaching sales to my seminar and workshop groups, I decided to incorporate an in-person survey to begin their training. The assignment was to go to a public place like a mall or busy street with a clipboard in their hands, walk up to people and ask them if they would mind answering one question for a business survey. The question was, "When I say the word *salesperson*, what words come to mind?"

Now this wasn't an original idea of mine. Legend has it that it had been done years before by what was then called The New York Sales & Marketing Executive Association. The point of the survey was to make salespeople aware they had an image problem because most of the responses were derogatory. Responses would be words like *pushy, car sales, disinterested, not genuine, interested in one thing (themselves)*, and worse. There was some positive response, but the overwhelming majority was negative.

This was meant to be a wake-up call for my clients. From there we'd talk about focusing on providing value for the client, and how to provide it. I would teach them how to establish relationships and the value of knowing what questions to ask.

That was back in the eighties. What about now? Has the perception of salespeople changed for the better—or has it gotten worse? I suspect that if we did the same survey today, we'd get about the same results. What does that mean for you if you're a salesperson? The good news is it isn't going to take much to separate yourself from the herd. This is a great opportunity for you if you know how (or learn how) to focus on providing value for your customers. By value, I mean what the customer values—not what you value. It's been this way since the beginning of time, when someone made the very first sale.

Why the poor perception of salespeople? Why do so many of them fail? Why do so many new businesses fail? **I think fear is the number one reason.** Fear of failure, fear of not knowing how to make next months rent or car payment, fear of disappointing someone, fear of not making quota, fear of being fired, fear of so many things that are personal and yet in-common with human beings.

The question then is this: How do you deal with fear and still be a successful salesperson?

The answer is to focus on your clients. Focus on their needs and more importantly, their wants. Maybe it's a way to save them time or allow them to enjoy time with their families. Maybe it's a way to protect them—to help them with their fears. It could be a way to let them have what they always wanted and now can afford. Sometimes it means providing answers to their questions faster than anyone else ever cared to do. Often it's just letting them know you care about them as a human being.

The answer can be many things, but they all have one thing in common: Each is something your customer values enough to give you money in exchange. But you'll never know what they value unless they trust you enough to tell you. That doesn't happen to salespeople who are thought of as being pushy, disinterested, and only interested in making a buck.

And please, if you sell for a living and interact face-to-face or by phone with your customers, don't call yourself a marketing person just to avoid the word "sales." It might make you feel better and ignore bad associations, but you're still a salesperson. Become the best in the world.

Look in the mirror when you get up tomorrow and say, "I'm a salesperson. Today I will focus 100% on providing value to my clients. I will ask the right questions. I'll establish trust before I ever talk about my products and services. I will make a personal commitment to be the best at what I do. Success will be mine because of the *relationships* I establish with my customers."

Where's the Small Business Chiropractor?

If you're running or working for a small business, you're not alone. Typically, small business represents the largest portion of any community's business base. We provide over 50% of the gross national product and over 65% of all net new jobs.

Here are some statistics from the Small Business Association[22]:

- We create more than 50% of the United States' non-farm private domestic product.

- We form the majority of the 4.1 million minority-owned and 6.5 million women-owned companies.

- We generate 26% of all export value.

- We employ over 50% of the U.S. non-farm private sector workers.

[22]Small Business Association: http://www.sba.gov/

- We represent more than 25 million firms.
- We produce between 13 and 14 times as many patents per employee as large R&D firms.

If small businesses are the backbone of America, why do our politicians focus most of their efforts on bringing *big business* into our states and communities? Why do they give multi-million dollar concessions to large companies, but seldom support small business (except with their words)?

For that matter, how *do* you organize 25 million independent firms? Is it too much like herding cats? Are we our own worst enemy?

If we're the backbone, where's the chiropractor when we need one?

The Stinking Corpse

"There is nothing as difficult and as expensive, but also as futile, as trying to keep a corpse from stinking." I'm not sure who deserves the attribution for this quote (and it sounds Shakespearean) but I suspect it's from Peter Drucker.

I have spent a good bit of time reading the details of Wall Street financial giants, and this quote popped into my head. There's a very particular financial climate in the United States right now. The government is engaging in "bailouts" to save big businesses affected by the down economy, and popular opinion is split as to whether handing them money is a wise solution to the problem. Are we about to spending trillions of dollars to try and keep a corpse from stinking?

Perhaps now is the time to allow these businesses to fail (just as Lehman Brothers, a global financial services firm, was recently allowed to fail) and thus free up trillions of dollars to invest in an entirely new national initiative for the United States. I'm with Thomas Friedman and the new green economy he describes in his book.

In *Hot, Flat, and Crowded*[23] Friedman sets out the clean-technology breakthroughs we, and the world, will need. He shows that the Energy

[23]If you haven't read this book, I'm sure you can tell that I heartily recommend buying or borrowing a copy as soon as possible. I've already mentioned it twice!

Technology revolution will be both transformative and disruptive; and he explains why America must lead this revolution—with the first Green President and a Green New Deal, spurred by the Greenest Generation.

Entrepreneurs and business owners risk it all. In return, sometimes we win big and enjoy both monetary and personal rewards. Sometimes, we also lose it all–only to pick up the pieces and start all over again. The Wall Street bankers and hedge fund operators in this situation risk nothing of their own. And yet, they believe they're entitled to riches beyond what most people can comprehend. They also believe that we should bail them out when they fail–when their greed allows them to sacrifice all of us.

I'm a capitalist. But I'm also a realist. I am *very definitely* an entrepreneur. Nobody bails us out when we lose it all–even when it's due to unforeseen circumstances and beyond our control. Congress doesn't hold special sessions to pump billions into small businesses even though the economy we create is larger than these special interests.

I agree with Drucker; one should never squander resources on the already dead. It's time to stop trying to keep the Wall Street corpse from stinking. It is time to say "no" to rewarding failure. To do so is only encouraging–no, *promising*–to do more of the same.

I posted these thoughts on my blog, and I knew I was being a contrarian. I was curious what readers would say.

Nobody was pleased with the bailout. Some didn't want it to happen and said, let the chips fall where they may. Most people were either confused, fearful, or both. Some of the readers posted comments, but more wrote me directly to have a conversation. One was in the process of applying for a mortgage but had just put the process on hold.

I am afraid that the bailout I'm speaking of is necessary. The market reflects the feelings of the participants. If the majority are fearful, the market goes down. If the majority are upbeat, it goes up. Both scenarios often swing much further than makes financial sense. The point of the bailout is to buy time so that investors will get happy and start to buy again, banks will begin to lend, and housing will stabilize. It's all about confidence.

But our country is in need of more than a bailout. We're in need of real leadership in our government, our corporations, our schools and even our homes. We've always been a nation of risk takers and innovators who were willing to work hard for the American Dream. When did we stop believing in that dream? When did "Dumb Become Smart?" When did it become a good idea to use credit cards as a replacement for hard work?

We're overdue for a national initiative that will use the strengths, hopes and unique qualities of our citizens to rebuild our nation. It's time to find people who can lead us out of the national crisis which is bigger than today's financial mess.

It's time to stop borrowing and start building. Our country's greatest resource has always been our people. We need to put people back to work so that everyone sees that they can have the American Dream again.

A green economy would utilize American creativity, put people to work, give people hope for the future and, in the long run, save our home. We have all the pieces to make a green economy work—we just need the leaders and risk takers to step up.

Quit Living in Fear

Fear is a powerful motivator. It is also an equally powerful de-motivator. Millions of people today are living in fear, worried about losing their jobs, their homes, and their 401K's. But there is one group of people that have no such fear. *They know how to sell.*

At some point in their past they made a decision to sell their way through life. I made that decision in 1st grade when I was given a box of Christmas cards from the Catholic school I attended and told to go sell it to raise money for the school. I didn't have enough relatives who could buy my "quota" so I started knocking on doors. I was hooked the moment I realized that I could create business by selling my products or services.

Some of you reading this have had a similar "Aha" moment. It was then you realized that you would never have to depend upon someone else to discover your talents, to give you a job, or to promote you. From that moment on you realized you had the power to control your own future because you could choose to sell.

If you're in sales but still living with fear, it's time to assess the problem. Would you like a list of why you probably aren't as successful in sales as you want to be? It's going to be a short list.

You aren't listening.

Learn to listen–*really* listen. It's how you establish trust, rapport, and relationships. I can't say this enough. I watch and listen to salespeople every chance I get. Ninety-five percent of them still don't really listen. They think they've heard it all before. They don't want to "waste time" and feel like they need to "sell." They're preoccupied with themselves, and they're living in fear.

Listen. Create value. Follow through. Keep your word. Maintain the relationship. Listen more.

You'll never live in fear again.

I Hate Rejection

Salespeople hate rejection. Some end up quitting and changing careers because they can't deal with it. People will tell you not to take it personally–that it's just business.

Frankly, I always took sales rejection personally. While I knew I couldn't win them all, I also knew that in order to meet the standards I set for myself, I had to give as much value as possible to the prospective client. So when I lost, I took it personally–and I made sure I had done everything I possibly could have done to win the business.

I learned from my mistakes, and I found that learning from other people's mistakes was even better. I spent as much time as possible talking to successful salespeople. I made a point of meeting the top people in the country by going to lectures, workshops, and joining associations where I could meet them personally.

If I couldn't meet them or hear them in person, I bought their books and audio recordings, and worked hard to make sure my efforts in the future would be as successful as possible. You're darn right I took it personally! I knew I had let someone down who needed my services.

I still don't win them all, but I still haven't stopped learning. I think they go hand-in-hand.

Don't Blame the Market

I often notice that the response to difficult or overwhelming external circumstances is panic. Many see the glass half empty. Some hunker down, pulling back from spending on their businesses, and generally wait for the sky to fall. Of course it's only sensible to have appropriate alternative strategies for both your personal life and your business when you have concerns about the world around you. But are you using these fears as an excuse for failure?

I remember many times over the last 35 years when, if I had let myself be restricted by the events out of my control, I would never have gotten out of bed in the morning to go to work. Very few businesses fail because of a poor market. *Lots* of them fail because of poor marketing.

Too many people seize on bad news as justification for their lack of success—and their lack of even trying. Remember the territory I was given when I started in sales for 3M? It was a small county in northwest PA that had been decimated by steel plant closings. If I had listened to all the "smart guys" in the company, I would have *known* I couldn't succeed there. Instead, I went about meeting people and talking to them about their businesses. We talked about the positive attributes of the area. I got to know them as people and I built relationships.

You know what I learned during that time of double digit inflation, double digit interest rates and double digit unemployment? **Life still happens!** People still purchased houses. People opened new businesses. People still made things and people still bought things. I learned that if I engaged in good marketing and positive thinking, they bought from *me*. They bought enough for me to set new sales records for the company, out of that county that "wasn't any good!"

The salespeople and businesses that failed during those challenging economic times had bought into what other people were saying about the market. They bought into a justification for failure.

Don't fall into that trap! Next month–next year–there will be more calamities (just listen to all the talking heads on the network news). *It's how you think about them* and the *action you take* that will make all the difference.

This Too Shall Pass

I recently spoke to a friend who didn't have the slightest idea what was going on in the world right now–except that he could give me hourly stock market updates. He's fixated on the stock market, and all he sees around him now are problems and danger. He's a small business owner.

I also read a blog post by someone who claims to be an expert in email marketing. She started out by saying: "With the economy as difficult as it is right now, you're probably cutting back on your marketing spending–dramatically." I assumed she'd continue by telling people why that's a really stupid idea.

Instead, she went on to explain how you should tune up your email messages. I have no issue with tuning up email, but to assume that people already have or even should dramatically cut back on their marketing is extremely shortsighted.

I think a better message is this: "People and companies will spend money in tough economic times–but they need to see, hear, and feel something new. The same old story isn't going to work. The person with the new, better, and passionate story is going to win. Have faith and get your story out there–or crawl into a cave and wait this out."

At a particularly difficult time during my US Navy enlistment, I received a letter from my father. My father was a man of few words, but this time he included a story about a man who had gone through one extremely difficult trial after another in his life. No matter what happened, the man kept getting back up. He never climbed into a cave or quit–even though he had more than enough excuses. He had no family, but when he finally passed away his friends found a Latin inscription he'd carved into his fireplace mantle.

I don't remember the exact Latin words but the translation has always stayed with me:

This too shall pass.

Persistent Genius

There is one difference between people who succeed in business and those who fail:

Persistence.

Every entrepreneur, business owner, and sales and marketing professional can tell you stories about their own failures. I have plenty of my own. Persistence allows you to get back up and try again. Being a gifted genius might allow some people to become top achievers, but I'm willing to bet that behind most of the "genius" will be a whole lot of dogged persistence.

Learn from your failures. Learn from best in your field. Learn from people you trust.

And then persist.

Try Changing the Picture

You've probably heard how you're supposed to learn from the past and plan for the future, but live in the now. It's a great idea, but I've found that the "now" isn't always working for me.

In such situations, I find that I usually need to change the picture. For example, if I'm stuck or not happy with sales or business results, I find that, like a movie that isn't working, I need to change the scene, the actors, or most likely–the director. Myself!

Continuing to "film" the same scene over and over again without making any changes is likely to continue to get the same results. Expecting a different result without making changes is one definition of insanity!

One of the best ways to be able to "see" what needs to change is to literally walk away from the "movie set" for the day, and do something different. Do something you wouldn't normally do (or something you just haven't had time for).

Take a long hike, go swimming in an icy lake, go to a comedy club—just go do it. Afterwards, when you're relaxed and feeling good about yourself, ask yourself what needs to change. Go to someone you can trust to be honest with you and ask them for feedback about how you can change. Make sure whoever you ask knows you want to hear the truth and that you can handle it.

When you're not happy, when the "now" just isn't working, when you know that "this" isn't what you want—try changing the picture.

Poverty Mentality

When the economy gets difficult, it sometimes leads to small business owners changing their behavior and developing a poverty mentality.

What do I mean by poverty mentality?

I knew a successful businessman who always wanted a Mercedes—and he could easily have bought one. But he never did. He also would spend hours looking for the cheapest airline fare, the best price on office supplies and anything he considered a bargain. He worked almost every weekend and evening when he could have been enjoying his family, social activities and friends. That's what I mean by a poverty mentality.

Paying attention to costs is a good thing, but don't lose sight of the fact that you can't buy any more *time*. Money is a means to an end. Having the goal of dying with the biggest bank account is not any way to live. Working more hours just to give up the things you love is not good business or good living.

I believe that time is the best currency, and that spending time on family, friends and yourself is your best investment. Taking the afternoon off to go fishing with your kids or taking your spouse on a surprise trip to the ballpark is much better than spending it looking for cheaper airfare.

I haven't seen the man I described above in many years, but I hope he's finally bought the Mercedes.

"Trying Harder" Is Overrated

You've got to try harder!
If at first you don't succeed–try, try again!
Ever hear those words? I'll bet most of us have at some time in our life. Most of us heard them for the first time when we were kids.

Humans are obstinate and headstrong when it comes to doing something that doesn't work. Kids often get punished when their parents or teachers think they aren't trying hard enough. We learn to keep on trying harder and longer and more often.

What if you took the approach that if something isn't working for you that it might be time to try something else? Think about it. If you already know that something isn't working then anything else has a better chance of being successful. Now apply this thinking to your sales and marketing.

Try, try again only has a chance of working if you are trying something different.

Never Give Up

When I was 21 years old, I had the wonderful fortune of working alongside a man who was already considered a legend in his field. Later, the world would be introduced to him via a hit motion picture. His name was Carl Brashear, but I called him Chief–short for Master Chief Carl Maxie Brashear U.S.N. You may never have heard of him, but there is a good chance you've seen a movie or a TV program about his life. His life inspired the movie "Men of Honor" starring Cuba Gooding Jr. as Chief Brashear. It also stars Robert De Niro, Charlize Theron and Hal Holbrook.

But this isn't about the movie—you can check that out for yourself (and I recommend you rent it soon).

This story is about never giving up. Periodically, the media engages in a lot of talk about "how difficult business will be for some time." And you know what? If you believe that, then I can pretty much guarantee it will be—for you. But if you focus on a goal and tell yourself that you will never, ever give up, I can pretty much guarantee it will be a fine year—for you. So much of what happens in our lives has to do with what we believe, and what we value. Chief Brashear epitomized the belief that a person must never give up. Here is a little of his story:

When the Chief originally enlisted in early 1948, the Navy had barely been desegregated. After basic training he was assigned to an officer's mess hall as a steward who served meals and polished the officers' shoes. But he wanted something more in life, and while watching some divers working one day off an aircraft carrier, he decided that he was going to become a deep sea diver.

He applied to school but was told that there were no "colored" divers in the Navy. They were about to get their first, he responded. In 1954, he became the first African American to attend and graduate from the US Navy Diving & Salvage School. He later became a Master Diver and a Master Chief Petty Officer, the first in the Navy.

I met the Chief under strained circumstances. I was planning on being discharged from the Navy in November of 1970 after serving a little over three years. I wasn't supposed to be discharged until a year later, but I was one of thousands who qualified at that time for an early discharge. I was looking forward to starting my career as a photojournalist when out of the blue, I got new orders. It seemed the USS Recovery ARS-43 needed someone with my set of unique qualifications and rank (at least that's what my commanding officer told me). I wasn't getting out early. Instead, I was going to spend another year at sea—and I would most likely be going to the Mediterranean for six months of that time. I wasn't happy.

A few months after I had already reported to the Recovery, Chief Brashear got orders to report to the same ship to assume the role of Master Diver. It's funny how life works out, but the coincidence of us getting orders to the same ship would change my life. I wouldn't appreciate how much until years later.

Shortly after getting settled onboard, I started getting to know the people I'd be working with. One of them, a First Class diver by the name of George Caswell, brought me up to date on the life of Carl Brashear when we heard he was going to be the new Master Diver. He told me the story of how in 1966, Chief Brashear had been working on the USS Hoist. They were recovering a nuclear bomb that had been lost when two US planes collided while refueling near the Canary Islands. During operations a rigging line broke, and a metal pipe flew and stuck Chief Brashear's left leg below the knee –and nearly sheared it off. He spent the next two years rehabbing his leg, which had to be amputated. But instead of being discharged or taking a desk job, Chief Brashear was determined to be reinstated as a diver. In April 1968, he became the first amputee to be certified as a Navy Salvage & Rescue Deep Sea Diver. Two years later he and I were to meet up on the Recovery.

As I mentioned earlier, I wasn't particularly happy about having to serve another year at sea, but I made the best of it. I quickly gained the support of the operations officer to whom I reported, and my commanding officer. In fact, I was given permission to start a ship's newspaper as we were leaving for the Mediterranean. Putting out the newspaper gave me a creative outlet and I enjoyed it very much, since I had worked as a reporter and a photographer on a daily paper before enlisting. I typed on a manual typewriter and then ran it off on a ditto machine. The first few issues were mostly about the ports we were visiting with some current event news thrown in, but it wasn't long before I decided to start writing opinion pieces. We were somewhere off the coast of Italy when I wrote my opinion about the Vietnam War, President Nixon and the Uniform Code of Military Justice all in one issue.

As newspapers go, it caused one heck of a lot of furor. My operations officer told me it actually caused a shouting match at dinner that night in the officers' mess. The career men on board (including Chief Brashear) were not pleased by my opinions, and several shared their opinions of me *with* me. The next day the captain explained to me that as a US Navy Petty

Officer I was not allowed the freedom to express my opinions about either our commander-in-chief or the Uniform Code of Military Justice. I had made a statement that the term "military justice is an oxymoron," and I think it was this that wound them up the most. That was the end of the ship's paper.

That evening, after word of the newspaper's cancellation got out, I was on watch in the Combat Information Center (my office) when I got a knock on my locked door. Looking out the peephole I saw it was Chief Brashear. He had never visited me before, so I was pretty much expecting he had something to say about the newspaper–but he didn't mention it. He just said he'd been on the bridge and thought he'd stop in to chat. He then wondered if I would like to join him in the boatswain's locker (his office) after I got off duty–to "work out" with him. He had a look in his eye that told me I'd be out of my mind to accept that invitation. He was also apparently not amused by my opinions. I told him I didn't think I would be joining him, and he said "okay"–and that was the end of the discussion.

For the next few weeks I stayed clear of him, except when we had to work together. He ignored me except to give me a stare once in a while; call it détente. But then something happened that changed everything.

The ship was short on its quotient of officers on board. The result was that the commissioned officers had to stand 12 hours on and 12 hours off watches as Underway Officer of the Deck (UOOD). The UOOD is the person who gives the orders on the bridge while the ship is underway. It's his job to give navigation orders, avoid running into anything, and assure the safety of the ship and its sailors.

One day the operations officer was complaining about the watches when he flippantly said to me, "You should be standing UOOD watches, since you teach us anyway." It was true that part of my job was teaching new officers some of the things they had to know to qualify as an UOOD. I said I would be happy to do that–if the Navy ever decided to let an enlisted person run a ship underway. I didn't think any more about it.

Now, it so happened that the operations officer was a tenacious kind of researcher. He checked into all the regulations, and he found that there were *none* that said you actually had to be a commissioned officer to qualify as an underway officer of the deck. You only had to pass a written test and be certified by the captain. Somehow, he talked the captain into allowing me to take the test. I passed it and the next thing I knew, the captain had certified me as a UOOD and I was put on the watch rotation. In those days if we weren't off rescuing or salvaging, we usually spent time running drills and also shadowing Russian trawler "spy ships"–which made for some interesting watches as UOOD!

I was standing one of my first watches (it might have been the very first) when Chief Brashear came up to the bridge. We were going through the formal ritual of changing UOODs, which involved me stating, "This is Petty Officer Poole and I have the Deck and the Conn." I remember looking at Chief Brashear, who had a look of disbelief on his face. He had never seen an enlisted man be given the Deck or Conn underway. It was unheard of at that time.

The following day I found the Chief, once again, visiting my office to chat. He wanted to know how it came to be that I was standing a UOOD watch. He wanted to know how he could do the same thing. I told him that there wasn't any regulation that said he couldn't, and that he could take the same test I took as long as the captain was good with it. I told him I'd help him with the things he needed to know that he wasn't already familiar with, and a few weeks later Master Chief Brashear was certified as an Underway Officer of the Deck.

From that point on we started talking about our lives and our futures when one of us had a night watch and things were quiet on the bridge. I told him how I was going to continue in photojournalism or maybe even studio photography. He told me about his life since being born in Kentucky, the son of sharecroppers. He never once complained about the prejudice he faced in becoming a diver. He never bemoaned the loss of his leg. Instead, he talked about never giving up on your dreams and wanting to experience as much as possible in life. I learned that when he wanted to go to First Class Diver's School, he couldn't pass the first time because of the math, physics and chemistry needed. He had enlisted with only a grade school education. He enrolled in the Armed Forces Institute and worked for three years to master the necessary science skills. He got his GED and went back to First Class Diver's School, where he graduated third in his class.

He would get excited when I would talk about my future and he encouraged me to do everything and anything I wanted in life. He was one of the toughest men I have ever known, but he was tougher on himself than anyone else. He didn't know the meaning of "you can't do it" and he pushed himself to withstand mental, emotional and physical pain that would break most anyone else–because he couldn't accept giving up. He taught me a lot about not letting someone else take away your dreams.

Master Chief Brashear died of respiratory problems and heart failure in 2006. How a man with a heart as strong as his can die of heart failure is a mystery of nature. His son, Phillip Brashear, said at his funeral that even while dying, his father seemed unwilling to let go of a life built on determination. "Even though his lungs failed him, his heart was still beating." Carl Brashear showed us all what a human being is capable of accomplishing when he's faced with overwhelming odds. Think about that when you find yourself thinking about how it's going to be a "tough year" for business. Go rent the movie, "Men of Honor." You might find yourself saying, "Never give up."

Thriving in Today's Economy

If you take a look at the photo of me on the back cover, it's pretty obvious that I no longer need a hair stylist. However, I learned something interesting about the spa and hair business last week.

I was having lunch with a good friend. We were talking about business and the economy when she said, "The hairstylists and spas are really doing well right now."

I almost dropped the piece of sushi I was about to eat. She told me she'd heard it from several people she knows in the business. It seems that people are spending more money than ever on their hair, facials, pedicures, manicures, massage, coloring–you get the idea. These are discretionary services that nobody *has* to buy.

I asked my friend if she had any idea why this would be happening in an economy where people supposedly have no money to spend on such things.

She said the people in the business think that people want to feel better when things get difficult, and that they'll spend money to get what they want and feel they need. Many of the businesses she knows are expanding and offering more services, locations, and custom pampering.

This is Sales and Marketing 101. Find out what people want and need, and supply it. We have always had ups and downs in our economy (and we'll have plenty more in the future). Some businesses will thrive during a down period because they'll continue to invest in their marketing and sales.

Now is the time to pamper your customers. Make them feel good.

Give them what they **want** and **need!**

Economic Opportunity, One Bite at a Time

I was waiting for an elevator on the 4th floor of an office building when I noticed a young man dressed in the uniform of a locally owned chain of sandwich and hoagie shops waiting beside me. He was holding an armful of literature and bags from the store. I was curious as to what he was doing and since nobody else was waiting, I struck up a conversation.

It turned out that Mark was the manager and one of the owners of those sandwich stores. He said he was in the building "marketing." I asked him how the economy was affecting his business. He laughed and said it has never been better. I said to him, "I have to hear your story!"

Mark told me that many of his competitors were typical eat-in chains or locally owned diners and restaurants. They were all complaining about less people coming in for lunch. Mark said he figured people still eat, so they must be eating in the office. He said that his stores are among the few that deliver lunches every day.

He started going to all the local office complexes in the area and dropping off samples and coupons for free hoagies. He said his strategy was to find people who had never tried them before, and then keep them as customers by providing a great product and super customer service.

Business has never been better according to Mark. When a customer uses the coupon they almost always order more food for other people in the office. When the food is delivered, the driver leaves another coupon for a different special. And so he builds the relationship.

At the end of our conversation, Mark smiled and offered me a coupon for a free sandwich. I told him I'd look forward to giving them a try.

As he walked away I heard him whistling and although his back was to me, I knew he was smiling from ear to ear.

Some people see a recession.

Some people see opportunity.

Which person are you?

The Value Must Outweigh the Investment

Every time you or I decide to buy a service or a product, somewhere in the back of our minds a dialogue takes place. Most of the time if the purchase is small or a commodity we buy often, we don't even recognize the "self talk" that's going on. When it comes to making a major investment that might impact our bank account or our future, the chatter gets very loud. It usually comes down to one question that we ask ourselves: "Does the value of what I'm buying outweigh the investment?"

Being a visual person, I often think of the old fashioned beam and balance scales when making a major monetary decision. In that visualization, I put the cost on one side of the scale and what I perceive the value to be on the other. The value had better outweigh the cost!

Your customers and clients do the same thing when you ask them to purchase your product, your service or even your ideas. Perception is reality; they must perceive that what you're offering has enough value to offset their investment. Too many people try to sell someone on their ideas without ever having created enough value in the prospect's mind.

So the question is, "How do you create value?"

You begin by asking questions and listening. That's why we call our sales and marketing consulting program "Listen First–Sell Later." It's imperative to find out what people believe they want and need. Ask questions that begin with "Who, What, Why, When, Where and How." Sometimes these are called interrogative questions. I call them Value Development Questions. You may have heard them described as "The Six Honest Serving Men."

I always hesitate to use the term *interrogative*; you definitely don't want to "interrogate" people. You've read this far and you know the importance of relationships and trust in any kind of sales process. By developing the relationship first, you can maintain a conversational tone while building value. Also, by asking questions and creating value, you'll have created enough "weight" on one side of the scale to outweigh the costs and any possible objections. And remember, never start "selling" and offering solutions until you have really listened and gotten all the answers you need.

This will work for you whether you're selling multi-million dollar products, professional services–or selling an idea to your children.

The Six Honest Serving Men were memorialized by Rudyard Kipling. Part of a longer poem, these lines comprise part of the epigraph to Kipling's short story, The Elephant's Child."

> I keep six honest serving-men
> (They taught me all I knew);
> Their names are What and Why and When
> And How and Where and Who.

Buying (or Selling) Cheaper

Let's say your sales career is at a point where you feel stuck and you're thinking of changing companies or product lines. An old maxim:

It's just as difficult to make a large sale as it is a small one. Actually, my experience over a lifetime of selling is that it's usually *more difficult* to make the small one.

One of the main reasons for this is that at lower price points, people tend to shop on price! Alternately, higher priced items or services usually carry with them some intrinsic value or cachet that outweighs the issue of cost.

This can work for marketers who are setting prices. Very often when I work with a client I recommend *raising* prices... while communicating more clearly the *value*. People who are only interested in cost are probably not good potential customers for a small business. Small business is usually focused on providing better service and value, and that doesn't translate to cheaper prices.

Like my good friend, Marie, said yesterday: "I'm tired of buying stuff from big companies and being dissatisfied with the quality. This time I went to a local company who might have been more expensive, but they sold me exactly what I wanted. It's not worth my time and frustration driving around, wasting gas to save a buck–and in the end get less quality."

It's All About the Customer

It's in your best interests as a salesperson to make a sale that serves the customer in the best way possible–regardless of price point.

Too often, salespeople go for the small sale rather than provide a service or product that would serve the customer much better. They do it out of a fear of rejection, and a belief the customer won't want to spend the money.

This whole paradox has a lot to do with personal self-esteem. Here's a shortcut that will help you do a better job for your clients.

Think VALUE! Constantly ask yourself, "How can I provide value for this person or company?" Focus on providing value and stop focusing on the cost, your income, your survival, or anything else along those lines. It's not all about you.

It's all about the customer!

Risk

We're in the process of implementing a neighborhood watch where I live in northern Bucks County, PA. We recently had our first meeting to discuss the process, and by coincidence my step-daughter, Lisa, was visiting from New Jersey and sat in on the meeting that was held in our home.

The day after the meeting she asked me why it's so difficult to get people to participate (even when they say they will). It seemed like a "no brainer" to her. You want to have a safe neighborhood where you live, and working together is a great way to form social relationships. "What's the problem?" she asked.

The problem is that the community is very new, and everyone has moved into it from other areas. Many came for the schools, some to escape the hustle and bustle of the city, others for jobs. Here's what I told Lisa: I think the problem is that, besides living in the same neighborhood, nobody knows if they have anything in common. Joining a tribe[24] and taking a stand, (which is what the neighborhood watch is asking of them) means giving up some anonymity. It means taking a risk. It means investing time. It means breaking with the status quo.

These are the same thoughts that go through your clients' and customers' minds when you're trying to sell them your products and services. These are some of the questions a good marketer must also answer when designing a marketing program.

Everyone wants to know if the reward they'll receive when buying your service or product (or joining a neighborhood watch) is greater than the price they'll have to pay. You need to provide your customers with enough rewards to be more important than both the real and perceived investment you're asking them to make.

In the case of our neighborhood watch, we need to show our other neighbors that the rewards of a safe, crime and drug free neighborhood where people look out for one another is worth the investment of their time and the fear of "getting involved."

What about your clients? Will they have to switch companies to buy from you? Will they be paying more for your product or service than they

---

[24]Another reference to *Tribes: We Need You to Lead Us* by Seth Godin.

might elsewhere? What if you don't deliver on your promises? Should they take a risk on a new small business? Maybe they like you but worry what will happen if you leave the company. Isn't it just easier to maintain the status quo–even if it isn't really the best thing to do? At least they won't get fired for making the wrong decision.

Just what are you asking people to do, when they buy from you?

Can you provide enough rewards to outweigh the risk?

Do you?

Reward

A basic management principle is this:

What gets rewarded gets done.

Let's say you're trying to understand why a particular employee continues to behave in a manner that isn't in accordance with your company's standards. For example–a salesperson who never turns in his reports on time, or doesn't turn them in at all. Consider that this particular employee is also one of your best salespeople.

Odds are, you're turning a blind eye to his behavior because you don't want to lose or "upset" a key salesperson. The salesperson is behaving in this manner because the "reward" for *not* doing the report is greater than any reward (or pain) you as the manager are offering for the action you want. If you want to know why someone does something, look for the reward.

The same principle also applies to your marketing. If you want to encourage certain behaviors from your clients and customers, **reward the behavior you want**. If you want people to buy more than one of your software programs or book titles, offer them a "tool kit" that contains all the products at a discount. Or better yet, offer each product with a half-hour of free consulting.

If you want to raise more money for your charity, you'll need to reward people and make them a bigger part of your story than you ever have before. They will have to see, hear, and feel more "value" for their donation and support (especially in hard times).

The reward must be greater than the pain. When economic times are difficult, it takes a different kind of reward–or level of reward–to outweigh the pain people are feeling.

It's up to you to test your rewards. See what people respond to. People always want to know that they're getting a good deal, and that they've made the right decision. Better yet, make sure they know they've gotten a *great* deal–and that they could not have made a better decision.

Be creative! Economic conditions give you a perfect opportunity to build extremely strong and lasting business relationships. Choose your rewards wisely.

My Sales and Marketing Hero

My mom, Dorothy, is my sales and marketing role model. She started selling shoes even before I was born and over a career of 50 years, she continued to be the best shoe salesperson in the world. During those years she also was in management and was a buyer for shoes, but she never stopped working with her customers. She retired so many times the company stopped putting the paperwork through; they knew she'd miss her customers and come back.

I've never had to ask her about her formula for success because it was always on display when I watched her work:

- She loved what she did and she loved her customers.

- She made sure she always knew the latest fashions and the latest health news about shoes. That health news set her apart from ever one else–especially when it came to shoes for children.

- She knew what her customers liked and wanted, and she made them feel special when they were with her.

- She has never stopped learning. She was asking me for marketing tips and books up until the day she retired for real. She still uses a computer and email.

- She always wanted to be the best at what she did. Settling for anything less made no sense.

Here's the part you weren't expecting: My mom has been partially or totally deaf for much of that fifty year career.

She was one of the first people in the country to get a cochlear implant back in the eighties. She taught herself to read lips before that so she could work. We used to tease her and tell her she owed her success to the fact she could never hear her customers say "no."

Mom learned how to "listen" to her customers even though she couldn't hear them. How are you doing when it comes to listening to yours?

Man Eating Chicken–Film at Eleven

P.T. Barnum would be laughing and rolling on the floor if he were around today to see our current crop of political ads. Call it what you want–hype, spin, deceitful lying–the politicians believe the public is no more sophisticated now than back in the days when an enterprising retailer put a sign in his store window proclaiming "Man Eating Chicken." The window was blacked out so you had to look though a small circle that had been cleared. And, what did you see when you looked inside? It was a man sitting at a table, eating a piece of chicken.

For years marketers have said you have to "sell the sizzle," and sizzle worked. But when people learned that the sizzle had nothing of value behind it, they *stopped trusting the marketer.*

Have we finally learned that there must be substance behind the sizzle? Are we beginning to look behind the curtain, only to find that the Wizard is just another lost soul?

It's difficult to get anyone's attention these days, but getting their attention with hype, spin and deceit says much more about the marketer and his or her opinion of the public.

Mom always said that actions speak louder than words.

Are you saying one thing but doing another?

It's a Revolution

For the last couple of years I've been telling my clients that marketing is evolving very quickly, becoming a new type of marketing.

I no longer believe that's what led us to the "new marketing" we have now. Today, I tell them that it's not evolution we're dealing with. It's **revolution.**

There's a marketing revolution in media content, personalization, community-based collaboration and quantity. Ideas are created, personalized, and published through more and more channels every day. They are read, viewed, listened to and then recycled at an ever accelerating pace.

You can take advantage of the revolution, but you have to act in order to do so.

- Are you constantly adding to the richness of your website content?
- Do you have a blog?
- Do you communicate with your clients where they hang out?
- Do you give back to the online community?
- How many social networking sites do you visit?
- How many do you join?
- How many blogs do you read in a day?
- Are they the same ones that your clients read?
- Do you *know* what they read?
- What are you doing to serve your customers and prospects using this revolutionary marketing?

• What does the revolution mean to your life and to your company?
You need to know!

That Won't Work Here

If you only knew how many times I've been told, "Our company is different—that won't work here."

Marketers used to say, "Never discount or give away your product or service, because that makes it less valuable to people." I thought it made sense.

Then one day, about twenty years ago, I met a guy at a party who told me he was in the software business and needed some marketing advice. It seems he had a bunch of software products that he sold for very high prices, but he hadn't sold nearly as many copies as he thought he should.

The products were good, but so were the competitions'—and pricing was similar. He told me he actually made a lot more money from annual maintenance and upgrade fees than the actual product sale.

"Why don't you put the products into a suite," I said. "Offer a highly discounted price for buying the entire suite, and then make your profits on annual maintenance and upgrades?" It seemed like a simple solution. The cost of the development had already been spent and having them sit on a shelf wasn't helping income. After discussing the pros and cons, that's what he did. It worked very well.

Can you give away your product or service and make money? I say yes, especially if it has a lot of high repeat business, back-end or add-on sales potential. There is probably no scarcity for what you sell. Lots of other people sell it too. But you have your own remarkable, extraordinary, *unique* story about what you sell, or how you deliver it, or your service. It's important for you to make it easy for people to discover it! At the same time, you're establishing the makings of a long-term, profitable business relationship if you deliver what you promise.

It's easy for you to come up with a list of reasons why this won't work for you or your company. But what if a competitor comes up with a reason why it *will* work–*for them?*

A Little Revolution Now and Again Is a Good Thing

Good isn't good enough anymore. It hasn't been for some time. If you work for or own a good company with good products and good service, you will lose out to competitors who have built (or are building) *remarkable* companies and products with *extraordinary* service. People have too many choices today; remarkable and extraordinary win in the long-term.

The good news is that I see more and more companies that "get it." They're moving toward remarkable. If they can't be the best in their own niche, they're finding other areas of opportunity. It can be painful, but sometimes you have to quit in order to find it for yourself.

On the other hand, I also see many companies that don't "get it" employing the same old marketing tactics. They're stuck with the idea of doing print and TV ads, direct mail, trade shows, telemarketing and cold calling as a way to tell their story. These are all outbound techniques which rely on interrupting your customers and prospects. It just isn't working anymore.

You need to be doing *inbound* marketing. Search engine optimization, blogging, social media, RSS, free tools and trials, public relations, white papers, landing pages, eBooks and more are where you need to focus your efforts. People who ignore this "new marketing" do so at their own peril and usually fall into one of three groups: the ones who don't know much of anything about it, the ones who are interested but don't know how or where to start, and the ones who don't believe it can bring anything to their type of business.

The first two groups can easily solve their problems by educating themselves or hiring someone who does know what to do and can teach you. The last group, truth be told, wants to grow their company but doesn't want to go through the rigors of getting there.

It's time to join the revolution. As Thomas Jefferson (or was it Sean Connery?) once said:

"A little revolution now and then is a good thing."

Create Connections, Content, Copy, Customers

The marketing rules have changed, but one rule that *hasn't* is that you still have to create great content.

You need to have something of interest to say. I like providing information, education, consultation, advice. I suggest you tell your story by–well–*telling a story*. People like stories, and they also like story tellers. Even if you're marketing really mundane, yawn inducing products, you can tell a story with some emotion. I have a golfing buddy who sells washers–and not the kind you use to clean clothes. (I know this sounds like a John Candy movie.) I'm willing to bet he can tell a story about how his washers saved the day in some commercial application.

We can all create and tell stories that are entertaining, educational, and emotional. If you don't know how to write good stories, then get a book, take a class, or outsource your ideas to a professional copywriter. The greatest ads ever written back in the day of print advertising all told a story. People didn't mind being interrupted by them because they were engaged in the story.

You need to do the same thing today–only you use different media. The money you spend on creating content for inbound, social media marketing will be less than you've been spending on outbound marketing using advertising, direct mail, or telemarketing.

Take small steps to build relationships. Think of it as dating, with flowers and candy. Give them *free* white papers, eBooks, and ideas. When they accept those, ask permission for the next "date." You can do that in many ways but one great method is to include another offer in your offer. For example, you can a link to a landing page with more information.

The more someone connects with you, the more interest they have in what you're saying and marketing.

What did you do today, to connect with your customers?

Practice or Preach

Practice works better than preaching–especially in light of the marketing revolution. For your words to have any meaning, they *must* be based on what you do and not only on what you say.

The decisions you make in regards to your employees (practice) are much clearer than what you say to them (preaching). The practice shows the real beliefs and values of your company or organization. You can tell people that they're respected and valued members of the team, but if the rewards, pay, promotions, terminations, and appreciation aren't done with respect and integrity, the company will lose respect, value and trust.

Your mission statement can be a work of art that is meant to convey exactly what the organization believes in and strives to meet. But if it sits in a desk drawer gathering dust, if it isn't *practiced*–it's useless.

You can write glowing marketing copy, produce beautiful websites, engage in social media marketing and do everything right according to the latest marketing gurus. But if you don't actually *deliver* on what you promise in the copy and what you say online, you're wasting *all* the effort that went into the "preaching."

Here's a true example of this kind of preaching: A well-known suburban hospital near my home proudly advertises the open MRI they have in addition to their closed one. Since insurance companies dictate where you must receive certain tests, doctors attached to the hospital must send their patients there for MRIs. But if you call to make an appointment at the *open MRI*, the hospital won't schedule you until you fail in your ability to have a closed MRI. "Even if you've experienced a failed one someplace else due to claustrophobia, you have to fail one with us first," a staff member said about their MRI scheduling policy.

When pressed for the reason for such a stupid policy, it turns out they don't really own the open one, and they make less money when they have to use it. So they make claustrophobic patients suffer through panic attacks and waste considerable time before they'll "allow" the patient to use the open MRI. I assume they get paid for the failed test by insurance, thereby making up the loss of income from sending patients to the more expensive one. Everyone wins—except the patient. And the patient loses trust in the hospital and the medical system.

It really is better to spend more time doing what you say than saying what you do.

More organizations should practice it.

Happy Birthday Joann

That's what the outside of the card said when I got it from the mailbox. It was decorated with balloons, a cake and candles. At first I ignored it, but then I did a double take. Joann is my wife so I assumed the card was sent to the right address. But her birthday isn't until December and this was July!

I gave her the card and said, "Happy Birthday!"

She looked at me like I had started cocktail hour a little too soon. Then she looked at the card, and started laughing. Upon opening it she said, "It's from Marriott."

After really looking at this bulk direct mail piece, we realized that it wasn't from Marriott Corporation at all, but most people getting it might have thought so. "Marriott" was at the top of the mailing, and Red Lobster and the Olive Garden logos were at the bottom. "In honor of Joann's birthday," the mailing said (I guess the one she would have in *five months*), "we would like to offer you a complimentary Marriott Weekender Vacation." (There's that Marriott name again.)

It went on to offer free this and free that from Red Lobster and the Olive Garden. "Our records indicate if you respond within 72 hours, you will also receive $100 in Gas Vouchers."

Inside was a tear off ticket that looked like a boarding pass –complete with bar code, room type (pool view king, of course) and even the room number: 1068.

Wow! This was a pretty amazing ticket, since upon further examination we discovered that the offer was good at over 200 Marriott Hotels. How did they manage to get the same room number at over 200 hotels? This was quite an offer!

In small type on the back of the "boarding pass" were the "rules" for collecting on this fantastic birthday gift. The one that caught my eye stated, "When you visit you *will* attend a vacation timeshare seminar lasting approximately 90 minutes."

That was *will attend*. Not *may*. Not *be invited*. Not *please!* I felt like I'd suddenly been transported into an old Hogan's Heroes episode, and Colonel Klink was passing out orders.

Then I noticed that in tiny print, at the bottom of the birthday gift, was a note that said:

"This promotion is not sponsored by or affiliated with Marriott but is a major supplier of VIP."

Personally, I don't have a clue who or what VIP is supposed to be. I guess I should know, based on the language in this gift. I'm going to hazard a guess that nobody else who gets this has a clue what VIP is either.

This is an example of the absolute worst kind of marketing.

What are Marriott, Red Lobster and the Olive Garden thinking by allowing their brands to be associated with something this slimy? You can put all the disclaimers in the world on it but it's still so slimy I want to go take a shower after reading it.

Please don't ever even *think* of using these kinds of tactics and interruption marketing. Spend your marketing dollars establishing a relationship with your prospects. Spend your money getting permission from the people you really want to talk with–instead of insulting people with this kind of promotion.

The back of the mailing says that a deposit is required to collect your gift. It ends with one of the all time great weasel phrases...

Some Restrictions May Apply.

Guess Who's Starting a New Business?

Lots of people, according to my friends Keith and Cheryl! They own a small print shop.[25] Business has been booming this year, and a lot of it is due to new customers. Some of these new customers have lost their jobs in the latest corporate downsizing; others have opted out of the big company rat race to run their own business.

Did you know that lots of new companies need your help–need your products and services?

How do you find them? And how do they find you?

Are you out speaking to every group of people within your personal niche–the people in your hive? Do you make a point to get out to local meetings and network? Have you asked your accountant, attorney, plumber, physician, dentist and customers for referrals? Are you reading the local papers to see if they mention new businesses starting up?

Are you applying what you read here, and what you read in other books or blogs? Are you asking for permission to stay in touch? Are you providing the people who say "yes" with something of value?

Keith and Cheryl opted out of very successful corporate careers a few years ago to start their printing company–and they've done all of these things and more. That's how they've grown during tough times. New business owners need your products and services.

It's your turn to grow.

Could You Be Treating Customers This Way?

I know this kind of customer service still exists, but I'm always amazed when I hear about it. A friend told me that one of her employees came into her office in tears of frustration and anger yesterday. It seems that this woman had just gotten off the phone with the phone company. Her babysitter had used a cell phone to call her, to let her know that her home phone line was out. This woman called the phone company repair office,

[25]Keith and Cheryl Messum own and operate a Minuteman Press franchise: http://www.eagleville.minutemanpress.com/

but she was told that it would take a *week* to repair her line. "That's not acceptable," she told the phone company. "I'm a single mom with children at home, and I need my phone in case of an emergency."

The phone company's answer, from the employee she spoke with: "We're very busy. We have lots of other customers who also have problems. It will take a week, and that's as soon as I can schedule it."

That was the end of the conversation–no discussion. What the customer heard is, "I don't care about you, your family or your concern about an emergency."

Maybe the phone company *is* busy. Everyone is busy. But in the meantime, the customer is worried about what might happen to her family without phone service, should an emergency occur. She was treated with disrespect and callousness. That phone company employee (and the person who wrote the policy) should be counseled into another vocation–one that doesn't deal with people or animals.

Could this same thing happen in your business? Don't fool yourself–it might already be happening.

Do yourself and your business a favor. Have someone you trust *be* one of your customers. Have them interact with your employees in different manners, like being ticked off or even angry.

See if your employees respond in kind or with kindness.

Check Your Expiration Date

What if we all were born with expiration dates?

Actually we are–but very few ever learn their exact date. So how would our lives change if we were given a stamped expiration date on our birthday?

Would you plan more or would you live your life more carefree? Would you live your life with more passion? I know people who live their lives like they know this might be their last day–and they do it day after day. They refuse to take part in a recession, or pity parties that last longer than 3 minutes.

I also know people who live as if they have forever and don't mind wasting today on being miserable and self-defeating. They also do it day-after-day. In business, you'll find them paralyzed by listening to all the gloom and doomsday discussion. Their lives become ones of self-fulfilling prophecy.

Which type of person do you prefer being around?

Which type are you?

Think about that as you check your expiration date.

Sucking Black Holes

Have you ever walked into a retail store, restaurant, or even a corporate setting and experienced the feeling that there's a black hole somewhere on the premises, sucking the life out of the place?

Your surroundings may be clean, with new fixtures and furniture. The lighting may be fine–sometimes even artistic. All the "things" in the place may be perfect. But there's something that just makes you feel unwelcome. It's something that makes you want to get in, and get out.

There's a retail seafood store near me. I had heard they sold great seafood, and I decided to make my first visit. It fit the description above–clean, well lit, with nice looking cases of good looking fish, scallops and shrimp.

But something was wrong. It didn't feel right. I watched the customers ahead of me being waited upon and then I realized: The cause of the black hole was behind the counter. There were several employees working, but one of them was miserable. She never made eye contact and every time someone wanted to add another product to their order, she gave a big sigh. It was as if she was saying to everyone, "If only you would go away, my life would be better."

I could see that the other clerks were being sucked into the hole. Even if they wanted to have a conversation with their customers, this miserable person would interrupt and sigh more. When it was my turn to be waited upon, I engaged a different young clerk and said hello. I told her it was my first visit to their store. She smiled and thanked me. I then asked if she could tell me about a few things, as some of the fish were new to me and I wanted to get an idea of how they might taste. "Sure," she smiled. I asked about types of scallops–whereupon the "black hole" jumped in and gave some abrupt answer to my question. Obviously, I was violating a rule (no questions). She did this even while she was handling another customer.

"I'm sorry," I looked at her and said, "but I wasn't speaking to you–and this young lady is doing an excellent job in helping me." I shot her my most withering glance.

She stayed away for the rest of my visit.

I couldn't imagine how someone could allow an employee to poison an entire store. The only thing that made sense was that she was the owner. I asked my young clerk who owned the store. She pointed out a man in the back, busy cutting up tuna. He heard our conversation, glanced up and made eye contact.

"You have a very nice store," I said to him. "It's my first visit."

He grunted something unintelligible and turned away, then disappeared further back into the store. End of conversation.

End of my visit–my first and last visit.

Do you have a black hole sucking the life out of your company?

Could it be you?

Encourage Leadership

As you understand by now, you can easily take the temperature of the success of a business by watching and listening to its employees. (Well, maybe you can't if you're the boss. And you might get filtered information if you try!)

The next best thing is to hire or ask someone you trust to do it for you. It's easy if it's a retail business–but you can do the same thing in any kind of business. Have someone pose as a customer. Restaurants do it all the time, but I heartily recommend it to all businesses. Do it on a regular basis. It will keep you from turning out like this:

There's a supermarket near me that should have a sign over the door to the employees break room. It should say, "Through these doors walk the unhappiest, most miserable employees in the world."

This is a business that has a culture and environment where people hate working. They have a lot of turnover. If you pass the staff walking around the store, they won't make eye contact with you. They're rude and only seem to talk to each other. Civility and good manners just don't exist.

You would think that ownership or management would have a clue to what's going on here, but apparently the employees have determined that it's the managers and owners who are the enemy. I have purposefully engaged some of the employees and gotten smiles; they'll talk to me. When I tease them about smiling, they'll say something like, "You wouldn't smile either if you had to work here for these people."

The last time I shopped there, I watched a check out line that people kept leaving for some reason—even though it was open and nobody was waiting. I *had* to find out why, so I got into the line. The clerk told me it might be a while as the lady he had been checking out was thirty-five cents short and she had gone out to her car to find some change.

"Are you saying you've stopped an entire line from checking out on your busiest day because she didn't have thirty-five cents?" I asked. "Did she pay you what she owed you besides the thirty-five cents?"

He said that she had.

"Why didn't you just ring her out and forget the thirty-five cents, or call a manager over?" I asked "I'm sure he would have told her to bring it later."

He said he couldn't do that—store policy.

"Here's 35 cents," I said. "When she comes back, give her the groceries. Meanwhile, you can finish ringing her out and check me out, too."

The woman in question came back before I left, and the clerk told her I had paid the thirty-five cents. She seemed very flustered and must have been combing her car to find lost change. I felt badly for her–and I told her the same thing has happened to me.

This is an example of a business with managers but no leaders. Don't allow your financial people to make store policy. Allow front line people to make common sense decisions. Reward them for it.

Are Millions of People Unable to Read Your Website?

By now you've heard of Firefox; it's a web browser from Mozilla. Browser statistics from an independent site show that over 40% of the web browsing world uses Firefox.[26] Six months ago they had over *125 million users*, and they just released a new version (which is awesome–if you can say that about a web browser). When this version was released, eight million people downloaded it in *one day*.

Here's the reason I'm telling you this: Wouldn't you think that a company the size of Sears would *know* about Firefox? If you were Sears and you didn't want to lose 40% of web browser users, you would make sure your website worked with Firefox, wouldn't you?

That's 125 million people! And when they go to buy parts from your site, they'll find something that looks like a big mistake. It is a big mistake–on the part of Sears.

You see, they only tested their parts site with Internet Explorer. It works fine there. But because they didn't take some extra time to make sure the site worked with all browsers, they turned off 40% of the internet.

How about your company? Have you downloaded Firefox to make sure all your web pages work there? (What about other browsers?) If not, you're making a big mistake and you're losing money. It's easy to get your site working fine with both browsers. If this isn't taken care of, someone in charge just isn't doing their job. If that's the case, you're probably using an amateur site designer.

Check your site now. Download Firefox[27] and test your web pages–especially the interactive ones.

(After writing about this problem on my blog, someone at Sears Direct Parts got the message and fixed their website within 24 hours. It now works just fine with Mozilla. You would have thought they might have said thanks!)

---

[26]All you ever wanted to know about browser statistics: http://www.w3schools.com/browsers/browsers_stats.asp

[27]Download Firefox here: http://www.mozilla.com/en-US/

"Google Alert" Alert

If you're not using Google Alerts,[28] you need to be. Google Alerts is a free service from Google that allows you to track any kind of information—news, articles, people, and companies—on the internet. The alerts are in real time (not historic), and you get a notification when the information you request appears on a page that Google indexes.

Since I do a lot of writing, I want to know who might be reprinting articles of mine in the press. So I track my name and certain articles. I also track any mention of my blog, website and two trademarked names that I own. Every day, Google delivers any mention of my requested alerts to my desktop.

If someone in Korea reprints an article that I wrote, I can drop them a note and thank them to begin developing a relationship. (This has actually happened.)

You could use Google Alerts to track your competition, keep up on news and developments within your industry, or make sure you don't miss any news about a product or service. Of course, you can also track your company, yourself, and whatever else you want. It's all based on your choices and queries. Signing up and using the service could not be simpler.

Give it a try. You never know what people might be saying about you!

Is Anybody Listening?

Last year I decided to switch accounting software and install Intuit's ubiquitous QuickBooks.[29] After installation, I wanted to watch the tutorial—but every time I clicked on it, I got a message saying I needed Adobe Flash installed (even though it *was* installed). I actually uninstalled it and reinstalled twice. Both times I got the same error.

I finally found a QuickBooks user forum where I discovered that everybody with version 2008 was having the exact same problem. *Adobe* had figured out how to fix it and gave the users instructions—even though it was a problem with Intuit's software.

[28]Sign up for Google Alerts here: http://www.google.com/alerts
[29]Intuit's QuickBooks website: http://quickbooks.intuit.com/

One post on the forum jumped out at me. The person said, "Doesn't anyone at Intuit read their own forums or listen to their users?" It went on to describe how this had been a problem for months, that Intuit already knew about it but had done nothing to fix it. *Does* anyone at Intuit listen? I wondered. The people on their forum don't think so, based on the fact that they haven't fixed an easy bug (not even months later).

I was going to write them an email, but when I started looking for the address I found a note from Intuit customer service. They were extremely busy, it said. They might not get to me for a while.

Two Bases

People need a reason to do business with you, and not *just* when you make them an overwhelming offer. You want them to forget to even think of the competition, or doing business with anyone else. You want them to have a personal relationship with you.

I drive over twenty minutes to my dry cleaner, passing at least eight others. They're in an area where I have no other business, so it becomes a *forty* minute round trip for the sole purpose of buying from this one store. I first chose them over ten years ago because I lived near them. Eight years ago, I moved.

I keep going to this dry cleaner because I have a relationship with the owners—a husband and wife. They deliver fantastic service. They remember my birthday. They go the extra step to help me out. One time I needed a suit, and I found out they were closing before I could get there. No problem, they said. They offered to bring it to me! The next time I went into the store, the wife said, "We had no idea you drive so far to us! We're going to give you a discount on all your cleaning from now on."

I would feel *guilty* going to someone else.

Some businesses have customer bases. Some businesses have relationship bases. One base will allow you to grow, to be profitable, and to be uninfluenced by economic downturns.

Which do you have?

Turn Off the Email, Turn On the Phone

What would you do if you opened up your email box tomorrow morning and it was empty?

You'd probably assume the email server or the ISP is having problems. But what if everything technical was working? What if it were true that *nobody* had sent you any email in the last 24 hours?

Would you say "Hallelujah!" and have an extremely productive day?

Would you quickly compute the amount of time today that you'd now be able to devote toward—oh, how about that exercise program you keep promising to start?

Or would you start asking friends to send test emails—just to make sure things were working?

I have many people who tell me that they get an average of 150 or 200 or 300 emails a day. They say it with an eye roll and a sigh, but I always wonder why they tell me how many they get. It's always unsolicited information on their part, usually during a discussion about the workplace.

I think they protest too much. I've come to believe that some people attach a level of self-worth to the number of emails they get. If you get hundreds of emails, you must be very important. Right?

Here's a program I use with clients that will make you feel good. More importantly, it will make your clients and customers feel good about you and your company.

Take one day a week and unplug from your email. If you feel yourself getting anxious about that idea, start with every other week first. Use an auto-response; it will automatically let everyone who sends you an email know that you're "unplugged," and that you'll be responding to emails the next day. Tell them they can phone you if it's urgent, and include your phone number.

Next, pick up the telephone. Call your top *ten clients* (or your top ten percent). Tell them that you want to know if you and your company are doing a good job for them. Ask them how you could do an even better job.

If they were in your shoes, what would they do to provide better (whatever it is you sell) for their customer?

That's all there is to it! Yet, nobody does this. Too many people hide behind their voicemail and use email with clients–so they can avoid talking to them. How crazy is that!

So go ahead. Shut down the email for one day, and pick up the phone. Get a headset so that you can keep on dialing and talking. Set a goal, a certain number of people you want to reach. Yes, you'll get sent to voicemail a lot of the time–but leave a message and I bet you'll get a call back. Have that conversation using the questions above to get started.

Keep track for the next few months. What happens with the customers you called? See if business doesn't increase! See if they don't send you referrals. And after you've computed the numbers, send a check to your favorite charity with some of the increased profits this is sure to produce.

A Laminated Thank You

When was the last time someone *really* thanked you for doing business with them? Can you remember? Did it leave an indelible impression?

A long time ago a very wise man and philanthropist told me that gratitude is the most fleeting of emotions. I'm not sure how this reflects on the human race, but I've come to agree with him.

What does that mean to you if you're in business, sales or marketing? It means you not only have to thank your customers and clients, but you have to do it often–and you need to do it in such a way as to leave a BIG impression.

Unfortunately, the most indelible thank you I've gotten recently is one that left a negative impression. I stayed at a hotel that has a frequent guest program, of which I'm a member. Their thanks consisted of two bottles of water and a letter from the General Manager on my bed, thanking me for being a frequent guest.

It was a form letter. It was laminated, so they could put it on the bed of the next guest they wanted to recognize. I didn't feel really appreciated. In fact, I felt unappreciated.

Who thinks up these ideas? Was there a meeting between management, sales and marketing, and someone from accounting snuck in? Do you really save a lot of time and money by laminating a frequent guest thank you letter for someone spending over $300 a night in NYC?

When was the last time you thanked your customers and left an indelible impression? Did you leave them smiling and feeling good about doing business with you? Or did you give them a laminated form letter?

After Every Sale

You should be sending your customers signs of your appreciation—a thank you note, a gift, flowers—after every sale. It's very simple, but few salespeople ever actually do it. Here's the key: You need to do it *immediately*. It should be sent the same day, or the following day at the latest.

Why? Well, there's the obvious need to say thank you. Just as important, though, is to reassure the client that they made the correct decision. Salespeople have a saying: It isn't really a sale until the check cashes. This will help get that check through the bank. It takes away buyer's remorse.

It's all part of building the long-term relationship you want and need. It's a simple thing to do.

Why aren't you doing it?

A Database of Life

Unless you've managed to lead a perfect life (or unless you're delusional!), there are probably things you wish you could do over. If there is one piece of advice I would offer anyone in business—something you should do now, not regret later—it's this: **Start compiling a database of every person you meet!**

With today's cheap computer power and software, there isn't any reason not to maintain a database of every person you meet, whether it's for business or social reasons. In fact, I don't consider those separate. I call this "My Life Database."

My first database was a bunch of business cards in a rubber band. Then I graduated to 3x5 cards and then more sophisticated card systems. But over the years many names got lost, or didn't get put into the new system. I kick myself when I go looking for a long lost name only to find it missing. These days, my database is digital.

Your database is really one of the most priceless assets you have in your business. It represents current relationships and potential relationships. Those relationships represent people who will do business with you, or refer business to you—but you need to stay in touch with them. Make sure your database has more than just their name, address and phone number. Know their spouses' and kids' names. Send them birthday cards. Find out their passions and interests, and drop them information you know will be of interest to them.

Business relationships must be maintained, just like personal relationships. Don't forget about a person after the dating period is over. Work to keep that relationship solid. A good database will help you do that for the rest of your life.

Get Out Your Pen

I have a box in my office storage cabinet where I keep letters I've received over the years. I happened to be looking for something in that cabinet Saturday when I came across it. I opened the box and started reading some of them again.

Why did I keep these, out of the many cards and letters I've received over the years? The answer to that is one of the best practices learned by highly successful people. Each saved card made me *feel good* when I first read it, and I very much appreciated the time the letter writer took to send it to me. I hadn't wanted to throw it away.

Email is a wonderful tool. However, taking the time to handwrite a letter, or adding a personal note to a printed letter, says you really care about your relationship with that person.

When's the last time you sent handwritten notes to your clients?

Remember Me and I'll Remember You

This is a simple idea, and one you can implement right away. Go through your customer files and sort for the top 20%–the ones who probably account for 80% of your business.

Then go to Amazing Mail[30] or Zazzle[31] and learn how you can send *one* customized postcard to each customer, with any photo or drawing on it, using your own text addresses. This goes to your customer by First-Class mail for around a buck! I've been using them for years and people love getting them–especially if *their* picture is on the front of the card. First they wonder how you were able to personalize it. Once they learn, many use it with their customers (and they'll have you to thank).

Write a personal message to them. Let them know you and your company want to help them. Maybe tell them how you've started a blog for your customers. You have started one–haven't you?

Give them a reason to talk to you–and remember you.

One More Thing

The postcards you can send from the vendors I mentioned can be very personal, especially if you use a custom handwriting font like I have.[32] And if you want to do one thing this week that will make a big difference in your marketing and sales efforts, make a commitment to send out three handwritten notes to clients, prospects, and friends–at least five times a week.

---

[30] Amazing Mail: http://www.amazingmail.com/

[31] Zazzle: http://www.zazzle.com

[32] You can get a custom handwriting font at FontGod: http://www.fontgod.com/

That's 15 notes a week! Do it for six months and you will have sent out approximately 375 cards. They can be thank you notes, renewing acquaintance notes, or notes that let someone know you're thinking of them and appreciate them.

You can write them while you're traveling (unless you're driving the car, in which case I rescind my advice). You can write them while you've got the game on TV. (Who really watches the whole game anyway?) You can find a few minutes each day to write them.

When I first started sending out notes to clients years ago, I made a habit of buying postcards during my travels. I'd write them out in the hotel in the evening. Sending them let people see where I was working, and they seemed to enjoy the postcards. Even if you don't travel, you can buy cards in your own city. Write a note about something you saw or heard on your trip that you thought would interest this particular client, and drop it in the mail.

I have my current cards made by a friend who owns a small digital printing company. You can have them made a few at a time these days, and the digital printing will make them look great. I get fantastic, creative envelopes at Envelope Mall.[33]

Find the time. I promise it will make all the difference in the world. You'll renew, enhance, and create new relationships. People will be shocked they got a handwritten note. In six months your network will be much wider and tighter. And, I'll be expecting a card from you then. My address is in the back of the book.

Giant Popcorn and Clients

Whether you're the owner of a small business, a sales rep working for someone else, or a partner in a large professional services firm, you can benefit from taking actions like the ones I've described so far. If you make a habit of doing these kinds of things, you'll be *recession proofing* your business.

---

[33] I love the Envelope Mall: http://www.envelopemall.com/

Here's one more: Just for fun, send your top clients **a giant box of popcorn.** They'll love it, and so will their entire office. You can even have the good folks at Giant Popcorn[34] insert a letter from you on your own letterhead–no extra charge.

Let your clients know that you're thinking of them. Thank them for their business and friendship. Ask how you can help them.

It's creative, it's fun, and it works.

Start Your Own Bagel Day

Speaking of fun, now is a great time to organize your company Bagel Day. Here's how it works:

Make a list of a dozen clients who know you well. Choose people you think will give you insight into how to improve your business.

Call them and ask if you can stop by to deliver bagels because you've declared tomorrow "Bagel Day." (If bagels aren't great where you live, you can substitute donuts.)

Every morning for the next two weeks, deliver bagels or donuts. That's all there is to it! You might want to take some fresh coffee and tea too. Don't forget the cream cheese. Thank them for being there for you.

A week later, pick up the phone and ask the same client–the one who signs the checks–if you can meet with her sometime soon. Tell her you'd love to pick her brain as to how she'd improve your business if she was in your shoes. Then put together a list of questions to get the conversation started. If there are some questions you're afraid to ask because you fear the answer, make sure you put them near *the top* of the list. (You definitely need to hear the answers to those.)

You'll learn some great things about your company and you'll walk away with ideas to implement. Your client will feel great that they're your client. They might even steal this idea. Let's hope so!

[34]Here's one place to buy Giant Popcorn:
http://www.cartsofchicago.com/giantpopcornbox/order.html

Selling Fun

Irvine Robbins passed away last year–he of Baskin-Robbins ice cream fame. As I read about his life, I got to thinking about something he said about what his company sells: "We sell fun, not just ice cream!"

Before he and his brother-in-law Burt Baskins opened the first store in 1948, the ice cream world was pretty much vanilla, chocolate or strawberry. Mr. Robbins decided to infuse his business with a little fun by offering 31 flavors of always changing products–with creative and crazy names.

If it weren't for him, we'd have no Rocky Road, Mint Chocolate Chip, or Cheesecake ice cream. Birthday parties at the store, clowns, balloons and a free taste of any flavor you wanted to try were all part of the fun he created.

What kind of fun are you building into your business? When is the last time you did something fun with your clients or customers?

Why don't you surprise your top ten clients this week and send them some Baskin-Robbins ice cream? Pick out some crazy fun flavors. Have it delivered by a clown or gorilla. Have some fun yourself, and put some fun into your business.

Your customers will remember this the next time they're tempted to switch companies. They'll remember the fun they had with you!

Create Your Own Wally World

Walt Zastawa is an old friend and mentor of mine. He likes to say, "Drop me off anywhere in the United States with only $20 to my name, and within a day I'll be making money."

Walt believes that even as a stranger in a place he's never seen, with no contacts, he would sell his way to success. He's a consummate salesperson. People buy from him because they like him and trust him, and they want to be part of his universe. They don't want to be left out of what I call "Wally World."

Why do Apple fanatics stand in line to buy the latest iPhone (or anything else that comes from the mind of Steve Jobs). Not everyone likes Steve, but they trust him and his ideas. Most importantly, they want to be part of the world he has created.

Do people buy from you and your company because they want to be part of your world? How much more successful would you and your company be if that was the case?

A Little Song, A Little Dance, A Little Seltzer Down Your Pants

I was talking with Walt a few days ago when I blurted out that I always felt like he was the only person in the world without a problem or care. Now I know that isn't likely, but his attitude and approach to each day has always made me feel that way. Walt's sense of humor is fantastic, and his presence is a constant reminder of the sheer value of fun in life.

Earlier I wrote about black holes. For every black hole person (one that sucks the energy out of a room) I believe there is a person who *creates* energy just by being nearby. Walt is such a person. People like this tend to have a great sense of humor, enjoy their interactions with others, and remember to keep some fun in their lives.

Here's a formula you might follow to become an energy creator:

1. Keep busy using your talents, and enjoy what you do.

2. Accept yourself as you are. Accept others as they are.

3. Set goals, write them down, and work toward meeting them.

4. Take the time to enjoy your goals when you do reach them.

5. Take care of your health and fitness.

6. Spend time with family and friends.

7. Learn a skill that has *nothing* to do with your job.

8. Develop the habit of reading both fiction and non-fiction.

9. Contribute to the happiness of others by focusing on providing value for them.

10. Never forget how to laugh. There's lots of value in "a little song, a little dance, a little seltzer down your pants!"

Honey Bees and a Trauma Center

Hospitals get bad press for a variety of things—malpractice, high costs, and sometimes callousness. However, one thing they don't get credit for is the *amazing* care they extend to people who have been severely injured.

Recently I happened to visit the trauma unit of a nearby hospital to see a friend who was injured in a motorcycle accident. She had to have surgery on a broken right femur and knee, and she'll be off her feet learning to walk again for a few months. She was lucky in many respects.

My friend had to leave the room for testing just as I got there, so I "hung out" and watched the activity around me. I noticed that everyone had a job to do, and while it looked chaotic and on the edge of being out of control—it was not! It was truly fascinating to watch.

It was much like watching a hive of bees doing their honey-making dance, while at the same time, each focusing on his own individual job. No one job seemed to be more important in the delivery of patient care than another, and all of the jobs were needed for both the care and the safety of the patient. I recognized that the delivery of hospital caring and healing is a highly choreographed process delivered over and over to get the best possible results for the patient.

Think about the processes in your company. Are they highly choreographed, with a vital role for each person? Are they actually chaotic and out of control? What would someone from "outside" the company say if they were to observe?

We need to re-evaluate our processes regularly to see if they're still working to create the best outcome for our clients, customers and patients.

Stop Managing

Out of the blue, I got an email from a guy who I served with in the Navy over 38 years ago. A while back, I had written about the small salvage ship we were both on and I had visited a website to get more information about what happened to the ship. He found my name there and sent me an email.

In the Navy, we were both the leading petty officers of our respective groups. He was an excellent manager and made a career in the Navy. I hated being a manager, and I left to start my own business. I liked leading my crew, but I never liked bureaucratic structure. I think that's probably true of most entrepreneurs and many small business owners. And that's okay.

The biggest business mistake I ever made was when I chose to manage employees instead of leading them. I hated that part of my job, and it showed. I was a terrible manager. I would much rather use ideas and passion to lead people than bureaucracy to manage them. I had forgotten that.

Which brings me to you: Are you managing, or are you leading? Do you have employees—a crowd without a leader? Or do you have followers who want to follow you?

My Navy friend reminded me of this lesson: Every day it gets easier to tighten your relationships with other people. Every day it gets easier to lead people—to have true fans that follow because they want to be part of something.

You're not going to be successful trying to "manage" your way through difficult economic times. You're going to have to create growth by creating change, and engage your followers. You can't push and threaten people into supporting you.

Take a look at the two 2008 U.S. presidential campaigns and you'll see great examples. One used change and created something people wanted to be a part of—something they wanted to follow. The other never had a consistent story, nor did he lead. He spent too much time pushing and threatening—managing.

So quit managing your business. Get passionate about your ideas, your company, and your products. Make sure they're remarkable and not boring. Boring doesn't grow. Ignore the critics. Just showing up isn't enough any more. *Lead* and you'll attract the kind of followers–employees–clients–customers you want.

Do what you believe in. People will follow.

Lead Them

In 1983 I wrote this paragraph as part of an article:

"I believe that one of the most potentially damaging myths to which business management falls prey is that superior marketing, advertising, or service is the answer to making a company successful. The truth is even the best of these things do only one thing for your company–they create prospective customers. The final solution to building and maintaining a successful business lies in the quality and capability of the people who communicate with and serve your customers."

Twenty-five years later, we're still learning the same lesson. Today's solution for many managers on how to weather the economic crisis is to terminate the people who communicate with and serve their customers. Big business is the worst offender! I believe it's because these companies are full of managers but extraordinarily lacking in leaders. Big business has too many hired guns who have no real stake in the company. It's not their money they risk. It's not their family who will suffer if they screw up. In fact, they won't even take the job without negotiating a severance package that will get them more money when they leave than they made while they were managing.

Small business owners can't afford this kind of management. Small businesses must have good leaders in order to thrive in a down economy. Leadership is *imperative* now. You can't lead people through fear. How can anyone trust a company that tells them how important they are to the company's success–when in reality they have one "reduction in personnel" after another?

Talented people are your most important asset. Identify them. Nurture them. Involve them. Inspire them.

It's Personal

Leadership is personal.

Because leadership is personal, your followers must trust you. But here's the real kicker–you have to trust others, too. That isn't as easy as it might sound. Withholding trust is a form of self-protection.

I've been engaged in entrepreneurial pursuits since I was a kid and started my first neighborhood errand business. I've gotten burned more times than I like to remember by people I trusted. But I've learned that in the long run, the only way to lead is to trust. You risk being deceived and let down, yes. But you can't lead by always wondering about the motives of those you work with.

You can't lead when you're afraid of being open to others.

People willingly follow you because of how you make them feel when they are around you. That's personal.

And *that* is trust.

I'll Say It Again

As a writer, sales and marketing consultant, and teacher, I like to think that once I've identified problems and offered solutions, my readers, clients, and students will rush out to implement the solutions–and everyone will win.

I learned a long time ago that this isn't what happens. There are a number of reasons. Just a few of them are:

- People don't agree with my assessment of the problem or the solution–or both.

- Inertia keeps people moving in the same direction they've been going.

- It's easier to keep doing the same thing (with a tweak here or there) and still expect different results.

- Not invented here: Some people feel "If it wasn't our idea, it isn't any good."

- It's easier to do nothing than to make a sharp turn–and fail.

- Some business executives are in love with their strategy and feel they'd be displaying weakness by changing their mind.

- My favorite: People get caught up with managing instead of leading.

Too many companies are well managed but poorly led. Some people spend all day putting out fires, organizing, and handling routine tasks and problems. Whether you're the CEO or a salesperson, other people in the organization will dump their problems and questions on you. Often, you take care of it on the spot. After all, someone has to do it. You're the smartest person in the room. The buck stops here. Who's going to do it if you don't?

But while you're managing, who is leading?

Find someone else to deal with the routine and then let them do it. I bet you know the perfect person right now to take that over.

Now you can concentrate on leading.

- Communicate your vision in a way that people can understand.

- Build trust by being consistent in your actions.

- Surround yourself with the best possible talent, and make sure they support your weaknesses.

- Listen to your heart and not just your head.

- Remember that everyone wants to be part of a community–a family–a tribe.

- The people you lead want to feel that what they're doing makes a difference to the tribe.

- They want to be led by someone who makes it exciting.

You can't do any of these things if you're managing.

So don't manage.

Lead.

What the World Needs Now

We need more leaders. Real leaders–people who are willing to "be the change we wish to see in the world."[35]

We need leaders who have a dream and can communicate it to others who are willing to follow–to make the dream come true. We need leaders in our homes and schools who encourage and nurture the creativity of children so that we'll *continue* to have leaders–instead of the functional illiterates that too many of our schools now turn out.

We need leaders who don't look the other way when they see cheating, lying, and stealing. We need leaders who don't believe something is okay just because "everybody else does it." We need leaders who refuse to be the kind of people who hurt others, using "it's only business" as their excuse. We need leaders with integrity, who can stop the bleeding of the million tiny cuts to our collective soul.

In a country where a man can be crushed to death by people rushing to buy gifts to "celebrate" a holiday of peace and love, we need leaders who can lead us away from greed.

We need business leaders who take responsibility for their actions. We need marketing leaders who use their talents to make life better by using the truth and by engendering trust from their clients and customers.

We need leaders who can and will change the world. We need leaders who listen first, before anything else. They're out there. You may be one of them. We're waiting for you. And, the world needs you–now.

---

[35]A quote from Gandhi. That and more information:
http://www.pbs.org/kcet/globaltribe/change/

Show Me the Love

Do you ever think about what you want for your customers, clients, and prospects? I believe the more you want the best for them, the more you build them up, the more generous you are with them, the more productive and successful you will be.

Seems pretty simple, and yet it doesn't happen often enough. People in business often get caught up in focusing on themselves – salespeople, marketers, business owners. Training and the ability to ask questions about a customer's needs aren't enough. You need to love them.

I think if you want the best for someone, if you are giving them your attention by listening, and if you are taking the time to understand them— you are engaging in a form of love.

If this is simple, why doesn't it happen enough? Fear is the reason. Fear of failure, fear of rejection, fear of loss, and more. But when you have faith in yourself, your message and your convictions—fear goes out the door.

Have faith and show them the love.

You Deserve to Be Extraordinary

Woody Allen says that 80% of success in life is "just showing up."

"Just showing up" isn't going to work anymore. It hasn't worked for some time, but as long as the status quo is maintained, people will think "just showing up" is good enough. Sorry, but it isn't—from here on out.

Today, you need to be extraordinary. You need to hire and retain extraordinary people. Your company, products, and services must be extraordinary. Your ability to listen to your customers must be extraordinary. Your interactions and communication with them need to be extraordinary, too.

"Take it or leave it" isn't going to work. The customer has many, many choices besides you. Interruption advertising won't work and neither will manipulative sales and marketing techniques.

You have one choice, and it's to be extraordinary.

In fact, that's just the beginning. Because you're only extraordinary if your clients, customers, and prospects *think* you are.

It's up to you to persuade them. Not by twisting their arms, but by *really listening* to them, connecting with them as human beings, and caring about what they have to say.

Your clients deserve it.

But don't forget that you do, too.

Notes

Page 15
http://sethgodin.typepad.com/seths_blog/2008/01/customers-that.html

Page 21
United Friends School: http://www.unitedfriendsschool.org/

Page 21
Ning, create your own social network: http://www.ning.com/

Page 22
Seth Godin used the term "sheepwalking" in his book *Tribes: We Need You to Lead Us*.

Page 31
Willie Sutton: http://en.wikipedia.org/wiki/Sutton%27s_law

Page 35
FontGod, make a font out of your handwriting: http://www.fontgod.com/

Page 40
From the book *Permission Marketing*, by Seth Godin.

Page 43
Hot, Flat and Crowded by Thomas Friedman is available on Amazon and from all major bookstores.

Page 50
All you want to know about The Piña Colada Song:
http://en.wikipedia.org/wiki/Escape_(Rupert_Holmes_song)

Page 53
"Greed is Good" from the film Wall Street.
http://en.wikipedia.org/wiki/Wall_Street_(film)

Page 55
The Federal Trade Commission and the National Do Not Call Registry:
https://www.donotcall.gov/

Page 59
My photography is online here: http://bobpoole.com/

Page 59
Mind mapping: http://en.wikipedia.org/wiki/Mind_map

Page 60
Stever Robbins is the Get-It-Done Guy™: http://getitdone.quickanddirtytips.com/

Page 63
Indiana Jones and the Last Crusade: http://www.imdb.com/title/tt0097576/

Page 66
This book was published using Lightning Source: http://www.lightningsource.com/

Page 68
American Business Media: http://www.americanbusinessmedia.com/

Page 69
Paul Gertner is one of the world's greatest magicians, and his website is here:
http://www.gertner.com/

Page 73
Toastmasters International: http://www.toastmasters.org/

Page 75
You can find more quotes from Lou Holtz here:
http://www.brainyquote.com/quotes/authors/l/lou_holtz.html

Page 79
The Best Seller by Ron Willingham can be bought used on Amazon.

Page 82
Small Business Association: http://www.sba.gov/

Page 83
If you haven't read this book, I'm sure you can tell that I heartily recommend buying
or borrowing a copy as soon as possible. I've already mentioned it twice!

Page 101
Another reference to *Tribes: We Need You to Lead Us* by Seth Godin.

Page 112
Keith and Cheryl Messum own and operate a Minuteman Press franchise:
http://www.eagleville.minutemanpress.com/

Page 117
All you ever wanted to know about browser statistics:
http://www.w3schools.com/browsers/browsers_stats.asp

Page 117
Download Firefox here: http://www.mozilla.com/en-US/

Page 118
Sign up for Google Alerts here: http://www.google.com/alerts

Page 188
Intuit's QuickBooks website: http://quickbooks.intuit.com/

Page 124
Amazing Mail: http://www.amazingmail.com/

Page 124
Zazzle: http://www.zazzle.com/

Page 124
As mentioned earlier, you can get a custom handwriting font at FontGod:
http://www.fontgod.com/

Page 125
I love the Envelope Mall: http://www.envelopemall.com/

Page 126
Here's one place to buy Giant Popcorn:
http://www.cartsofchicago.com/giantpopcornbox/order.html

Page 134
A quote from Gandhi. That and more information:
http://www.pbs.org/kcet/globaltribe/change/

Acknowledgements

This book is the result of the combined efforts of a host of people who have inspired and guided me throughout my life.

First, a million thanks to the tireless efforts of Megan Elizabeth Morris who used her wonderful editing skills and her brilliant intellect to make sense of my writing. If you ever write a book, you need a Magnificent Megan Morris in your corner.

Likewise, my thanks go out to Paul Durban who designed the cover and formatted this book. He is an extremely talented man and I am looking forward to working with he and Megan in the future.

I've been inspired by a number of people whose work I admire. Thank you to : Seth Godin, Malcolm Gladwell, Harry Beckwith, Ron Willingham, Katherine Radeka, Bill Brooks, Alan Weiss, Thomas L. Friedman, Harvey Mackay, Tom Peters, Jay Conrad Levinson, Mel and Patricia Ziegler, Bill Rosenzweig, Kevin Berchelmann, Stever Robbins, Richard Bandler, Peter F. Drucker, Kevin Kelly, Chris Brogan, Zig Ziglar and a host of others I'm going to kick myself for not remembering.

Over my lifetime I've had the privilege and honor of being able to learn directly from friends who taught me more than they can imagine. Heartfelt thanks to: Art Thomas, Beverly and Tim Walden, Bob Popp, Charlie Pasquine, Cheryl and Keith Messum, Christine and Shupei Chiao, Dave Taylor, David Greenwald, Don Eckert, Frank C. Dawson, Frank Mangano, George Caswell, Glen Waight, Greg Manning, Harry Stewart, Jack Lambert, Jack Reznicki, Jack Vodrey, Jeff Sweet, Jerry Nachman, Jill Chernekoff, Jim Calla, Jim Farris, John Milcoff, John Nack, Kathy and Stephen Redding, Kathy Duffy, Lou Holtz, Marie and Bob West, Mark McConnell, Martha Eberhardt, Master Chief Carl Brashear, Nancy Donnelly, Paul Gertner, Ray and Joe Trevelline, Rick Nasal, Rob Plotkin, Scott Ferrell, Sharon Moore, Tom Poff, and Walt and Becky Zastawa.

I belong to a wonderful group of talented, caring people at Triiibes. I can't name them all but I have to mention a few people whose wisdom has helped me. They are: Anne McCrossan, Barry Adams, Becky Blanton, Bernadette Jiwa, Bernd Nurnberger, Bodo Albrecht, Bonnie Larner, Char James-Tanney, Chris Sommovigo, David Trilling, Didier Daglinckx, Dr. Mani Sivasubramanian, Ed Welch, Ellen Di Resta, Jodi Kaplin, Joel Canfield, Jule Kucera, Keith Jennings, Pace and Kyeli Smith, Marcos Gaser, Martin Whitmore, Megan Morris, Michael Donk, Patrick Smith, Paul Durban, Richard Merrick, Stephen Snyder, Tiara Shafiq, Tom Bentley, and Trish Lambert

I also have the pleasure and privilege to serve as a coach to fellows of the WIN organization. WIN is the Greater Philadelphia region's only organization specifically for women who are leaders of and investors in high-growth businesses. WIN promotes the expansion of women-led and women-owned businesses with high growth potential through education, networking, mentoring, and exposure to investment resources.

And, a great big thank you to my family. Thank you Mom for showing me how to sell. Thank you Joann for teaching me how to listen.

Mindy and Ryan – you make me very proud!

And, finally, to my brother Dave and sisters Judy, Barbara and Stephanie, I appreciate all that you do for everyone. You're a wonderful family. Thanks for putting up with me!

Resource Guide

Recommended Business Books

How to Win Friends & Influence People by Dale Carnegie

Tribes by Seth Godin

On Becoming a Leader by Warren Bennis

The Essential Drucker by Peter Drucker

In Search of Excellence by Thomas J. Peters and Robert H. Waterman, Jr.

Million Dollar Consulting by Alan Weiss

Selling the Invisible by Harry Beckwith

Purple Cow by Seth Godin

Permission Marketing by Seth Godin

The Tipping Point by Malcolm Gladwell

Birth of a Salesman by Walter A. Friedman

Guerrilla Marketing by Jay Conrad Levinson

The Art of the Start by Guy Kawasaki

Positioning by Al Ries and Jack Trout

The Republic of Tea by Mel Ziegler, Patricia Ziegler, and Bill Rosenzweig

The E-Myth Revisited by Michael E. Gerber

Some Websites and Blogs I Like

My place to discuss sales, marketing and leadership.
http://www.pooleswatercooler.com/

Seth Godin is a bestselling author, entrepreneur and agent of change.
http://www.sethgodin.com/

Technology start-up blog.
http://www.techcrunch.com/

Shop, create or sell what's on your mind.
http://www.cafepress.com/

Buy and sell all things homemade.
http://www.etsy.com/

Create your own webpage in 60 seconds, earn money, and
support charity.
http://www.squidoo.com/

Each of us can make a difference.
http://dripit.org/

Social business media strategy and more.
http://www.chrisbrogan.com/

Personal revelations of the Magnificent Megan M.
http://worldmegan.net/

"We're on a mission to spread important ideas and change minds."
http://changethis.com/

Amazing ideas to make you think.
http://www.kk.org/thetechnium/

Writes about changing the world while he also goes about changing it.
http://www.danpink.com/

Starting a home based business.
http://ittybiz.com/

How to make ideas stick.
http://madetostick.com/

Author of *The Art of the Start*.
http://www.guykawasaki.com/

An outpost for curious divergent thinkers.
http://creativegeneralist.blogspot.com/

Women Inventing Next, where I serve as a mentor.
http://www.winwomen.org/

United Friends School, a special school in Quakertown, PA.
http://www.unitedfriendsschool.org

The Seed Vase Project: Connect the dots... we're all connected.
http://www.seedvase.blogspot.com/

World change starts with educated children.
http://www.roomtoread.org/

My address:

Bob@PooleConsultingGroup.com
Telephone Toll Free Number – 877-945-3837

Mailing address:

Bob Poole
31 Bryant Drive
Perkasie, PA 18944

Thank you very much for reading *Listen First–Sell Later*. Please send me your feedback. I particularly enjoy wonderful reviews but I'll listen to <u>everything</u> you have to say. I sincerely hope that some of what I've written will change the way you sell, communicate and, most importantly, listen to your family, friends and customers.

LaVergne, TN USA
09 June 2010
185574LV00001B/2/P